China's Financial System

Westview Replica Editions

The concept of Westview Replica Editions is a response to the continuing crisis in academic and informational publishing. Library budgets for books have been severely curtailed. Ever larger portions of general library budgets are being diverted from the purchase of books and used for data banks, computers, micromedia, and other methods of information retrieval. Interlibrary loan structures further reduce the edition sizes required to satisfy the needs of the scholarly community. Economic pressures on the university presses and the few private scholarly publishing companies have severely limited the capacity of the industry to properly serve the academic and research communities. As a result, many manuscripts dealing with important subjects, often representing the highest level of scholarship, are no longer economically viable publishing projects—or, if accepted for publication, are typically subject to lead times ranging from one to three years.

Westview Replica Editions are our practical solution to the problem. We accept a manuscript in camera-ready form, typed according to our specifications, and move it immediately into the production process. As always, the selection criteria include the importance of the subject, the work's contribution to scholarship, and its insight, originality of thought, and excellence of exposition. The responsibility for editing and proofreading lies with the author or sponsoring institution. We prepare chapter headings and display pages, file for copyright, and obtain Library of Congress Cataloging in Publication Data. A detailed manual contains simple instructions for preparing the final typescript, and our editorial staff is always available to answer questions.

The end result is a book printed on acid-free paper and bound in sturdy library-quality soft covers. We manufacture these books ourselves using equipment that does not require a lengthy make-ready process and that allows us to publish first editions of 300 to 600 copies and to reprint even smaller quantities as needed. Thus, we can produce Replica Editions quickly and can keep even very specialized books in print as long as there is a demand for them.

About the Book and Author

China's Financial System:
The Changing Role of Banks
William Byrd

Strengthening the banking system and expanding its role in resource mobilization and allocation have been key components of recent economic reform policies in the People's Republic of China. This study of China's financial system focuses on new policies and reforms undertaken since 1976, including institutional restoration, proliferation, and decentralization; enhancement of the position of banks vis-à-vis their clients; introduction of credit financing of fixed investment; rationalization of the structure of interest rates and strengthening their role in guiding economic decision making; and a new emphasis on the banking system as a true financial intermediary. Citing fundamental institutional weaknesses inherited from the period of the Cultural Revolution and its aftermath and pointing to contradictions between economic reforms and the prereform management system, Mr. Byrd concludes that the changes implemented thus far have had mixed results and suggests that it will be some time before the banking system can assume its proper position in the Chinese economy.

The book provides a detailed account of the institutional structure of China's financial and banking systems; a review of policy and performance in 1949-1976, the key features of post-Mao China's economic reform package, and developments in 1976-1982; an evaluation of the success of the main financial and banking reforms, especially in the area of investment financing; and an assessment of the prospects for the future.

William Byrd is a Ph.D. candidate in the department of economics at Harvard University.

China's Financial System
The Changing Role of Banks

William Byrd

Westview Press / Boulder, Colorado

A Westview Replica Edition

Copyright © 1983 by Westview Press, Inc.

Published in 1983 in the United States of America by
    Westview Press, Inc.
    5500 Central Avenue
    Boulder, Colorado 80301
    Frederick A. Praeger, President and Publisher

Library of Congress Cataloging in Publication Data

Byrd, William A. (William Anderson)
    China's financial system.

    (A Westview replica edition)
    Bibliography: p.
    1. Banks and banking--China. 2. Finance--China.
I. Title.
HG3334.B94 1983   332.1'0951   83-6610
ISBN 0-86531-943-X

Printed and bound in the United States of America.

10 9 8 7 6 5 4 3

may 85

Contents

List of Tables ix
Abbreviations x
Acknowledgments xi

1   INTRODUCTION. 1

2   INSTITUTIONAL FRAMEWORK 7

   The People's Bank of China. 8
   The Agricultural Bank of China and Rural
      Credit Cooperatives 14
   The Bank of China and Other Organs Involved
      in International Work 18
   The People's Insurance Company of China . . . 24
   The Ministry of Finance 25
   The People's Construction Bank of China . . . 28

3   POLICY AND PERFORMANCE, 1949-1976 31

   Basic Principles of Banking in a Command
      Economy 31
   Chinese Departures from the Soviet Model. . . 35
   Inflation Control 38
   Political and Specific Sectoral Objectives. . 41
   Efficiency in Allocation and Use of Working
      Capital Loans 44

4   BANKING REFORMS, 1976-1982: BACKGROUND AND
   CHRONOLOGICAL REVIEW. 49

   Background. 49
   Main Directions of Banking Reform 56
   Chronological Review. 58

5 EVALUATION OF MAIN BANKING REFORMS AND POLICY
   CHANGES   71

   Decentralization of the Credit Management
     System.   71
   Changes in the Structure of Interest
     Rates   75
   Institutional Reforms   78
   Financial Intermediation.   81
   Inflation Control   84

6 INVESTMENT FINANCING.   89

   Individual Savings.   90
   Bank Deposits of Organizations.   93
   Foreign Financing   94
   The State Budget.   96
   Extrabudgetary Funds.   97
   Self Financing.   101
   Direct Investment   102
   Efficiency of Investment.   106

7 EASTERN EUROPEAN BANKING REFORMS: THE LESSONS
   FOR CHINA   109

   Relationship Between Banking Reforms and
     Reforms in the Rest of the Economy.   111
   Financing of Fixed Investment   113
   Excessive Enterprise Liquidity.   115
   Credit Restrictions and Trade Credit.   116
   Financing of Circulating Capital.   118
   Institutional Reform.   118
   Foreign Debt.   119
   General Considerations.   120

8 CONCLUSIONS   123

   Institutional Changes   123
   Changes in the Structure of Interest Rates. . .   125
   Internal Decentralization of the Banking
     System.   125
   Fiscal Decentralization   126
   Loan Financing of Fixed Investment.   128
   Financial Intermediation.   128
   Main Patterns   129
   Prognosis   130

Tables   133
Abbreviations of Periodicals   165
Notes.   167
Bibliography   181

Tables

1. China's State Banking Statistics 134
2. Long-Term Growth Rates of Various Financial
   Aggregates 137
3. Deposits and Loans of Rural Credit
   Cooperatives 140
4. Bank of China Balance Sheet. 141
5. The People's Insurance Company of China
   1979 International Accounts. 144
6. State Budget Revenues. 147
7. State Budget Expenditures. 149
8. Average Wages in China's State Sector. . . . 151
9. Current Interest Rates on Loans and
   Deposits of Economic Units 152
10. Monthly Interest Rates on Individuals'
    Bank Deposits. 154
11. Historical Trend of Monthly Interest Rates
    on Various Types of Loans. 155
12. Individual Savings Deposits in China 157
13. Average Per Capita Individual Savings
    Deposits 159
14. Private Financial Savings as a Proportion
    of National Income 160
15. Urban Savings Rates. 161
16. Rural Savings Rates. 162
17. Source of Financing of State Capital
    Construction Investment. 163

Abbreviations

ABC	–	Agricultural Bank of China
BOC	–	Bank of China
CITIC	–	China International Trust and Investment Corporation
FICC	–	Foreign Investment Control Commission
GAFX	–	General Administration of Exchange Control
MOF	–	Ministry of Finance
PBC	–	People's Bank of China
PCBC	–	People's Construction Bank of China
PICC	–	People's Insurance Company of China
SCCC	–	State Capital Construction Commission
TTIC	–	Tianjin Trust and Investment Corporation

Acknowledgments

This study was originally drafted in the summer of 1981, based on research work done in that year. The manuscript was revised and updated in early 1983 to prepare it for publication. However, no substantial new ideas were added at that time. The analysis and information presented for the most part cover developments through the end of 1981. Available information on 1982 has been utilized in the discussion of certain topics.

As a PhD Candidate in the Department of Economics, Harvard University, I have received financial support in the form of Foreign Language and Area Studies (FLAS) awards and a Schumpeter Fellowship. Since these helped enable me to undertake this study, thanks are due to the Schumpeter Foundation of Harvard University and the US Department of Education, for their general support of my graduate studies in economics.

At various stages in its preparation this study has benefitted from the comments of a number of people, including Bela Balassa, Dwight Perkins, Carl Walter, and Christine Wong. Their help is gratefully acknowledged. Barry Naughton carefully read through and commented on several drafts of the manuscript, for which he deserves special thanks. Andrea Rogers and Cora Centeno undertook preparation of the final typescript for publication.

Responsibility for any remaining errors and omissions in this monograph is of course my own. The ideas and opinions expressed in this study reflect my personal views and should not be attributed to any other person or institution.

Lastly, my wife and son's patience were an essential ingredient in enabling me to complete this work. My thanks for their forbearance during the long months of research and writing.

William Byrd

1
Introduction

    In scholarly work on centrally planned economies
the financial sector often has received less attention
than it deserves. There are a number of reasons for
this. In the first place, quantitative data on money
and credit have in many cases not been published on a
regular basis by the countries concerned. Information
on the government budget also tends to be skimpy and
incomplete. However inadequate the statistics on the
real sectors of centrally planned economies, they are
generally far better than the financial statistics
available. Perhaps more important than data problems
in explaining the neglect of the financial sphere,
however, is the presumption that it is relatively
unimportant in explaining the performance and problems
of centrally planned economies - money in the state
sector is "passive;" credit has no independent role and
is largely determined by outside forces like inventory
accumulation. The government budget merely reflects
planning geared toward the real economy and has no
independent effect on firms' activities. All in all,
the financial sphere may be interesting, but it should
not be the main focus of scholarly research, because
the institutions and policy decisions that ultimately
affect economic performance are located elsewhere - in
the planning system and the administrative hierarchy
that supervises producers and other economic units.
    In China the first reason mentioned above is no
longer valid. Statistical information of relatively
good quality is now available on both the government
budget and the banking system (see Tables 1, 3, 6, and
7). In addition, considerable amounts of scattered
micro-level or provincial-level financial data are now
available in Chinese financial journals and books.[1]
There are still problems in understanding the data, its
scope, and precise definitions, as well as in analyzing

1

institutional interactions and decisionmaking processes. Even here, the great volume of published
Chinese work on the financial system now appearing is
very helpful. Availability of data is now much less of
a constraint hindering research on China's financial
system than it was in the past.

The second factor resulting in partial neglect of
the financial system in centrally planned economies
also does not apply in the case of China. Because of
the country's relatively weak planning system and
decentralized system of economic administration,
financial resources may have been more important in
affecting economic performance than in other centrally
planned economies all along. This does not mean that
the banking system itself has necessarily been in a
stronger position, but it does mean that financial
aspects have played a considerably more important role
(positive or negative) in the decisions of lower-level
units than they have in other centrally planned
economies. With the advent of economic reforms in the
late 1970s, the role of financial resources, institutions, and criteria has become even more important.
The point has been reached where neglect of financial
aspects in any detailed study of economic policies,
performance, and reforms in China would render such
work dangerously incomplete.

This monograph utilizes newly available information about China's financial system to further our
understanding of its institutional structure, its
interaction with the rest of the system of economic
planning and administration, and the impact of financial aggregates on the real sectors of the economy.
Large volumes of both quantitative and qualitative data
on the financial system as well as other sectors of the
Chinese economy are being published at a rapid rate. A
few of the milestones in this regard have been: (1)
the issuance of annual statistical reports by the State
Statistical Bureau starting in 1978; (2) the public
announcement of annual budgetary statistics and budget
plans, starting in 1979; (3) the resumption of publication of the People's Bank of China's monthly journal
Zhongguo Jinrong (China's Finance), starting in 1979;
(4) the publication of an economic yearbook in 1981,
followed by a second one in 1982; and (5) perhaps most
important, the publication of a comprehensive statistical yearbook in late 1982. Some of these and other
sources of information emerged as this study was being
written or after it was completed; thus they have by no
means been fully utilized.

Since it was written at just the time when information on the Chinese economy was rapidly growing in
quantity and greatly improving in quality, a work like
this runs the risk of becoming quickly outdated,

especially those parts of it dealing with the most recent reforms, policy changes, and quantitative developments. But this study attempts to get at underlying issues and problems, which will probably continue to affect China's financial system in the future, regardless of changes in concrete policy measures or quantitative relationships. Though our understanding of the Chinese economy in general and the financial sector in particular will continue to improve as more information is made available, our perception of the key issues and problems may not change greatly.

In its approach this study is institutional and policy-oriented. Understanding of the changing institutional framework and the main institutional-administrative relationships is a prerequisite for meaningful quantitative or theoretical analysis of China's financial system. Much of the discussion deals with changing policies and their impact on the financial system and the economy as a whole. This focus is appropriate since economic reforms in China are of recent origin and are still being implemented. The final results are not yet in, and policy-oriented analysis and evaluation by both Chinese and outside scholars may have some meaningful role to play, in pointing out which avenues have been successful enough to merit further exploration and which could prove to be dead ends.

Chapter 2 outlines the institutional structure of the Chinese financial system and presents available quantitative information. The institutional history of some of the main financial organizations is also briefly discussed. Chapter 2 should provide the basis for subsequent analysis of policies, reforms, and institutional changes.

Chapter 3 briefly reviews financial sector policies and performance from the founding of the People's Republic of China to the almost simultaneous death of Mao Zedong and downfall of the so-called "Gang of Four," which set the stage for subsequent reforms. It is impossible to do justice to a topic this vast in such a brief survey - the goal is rather the much more modest one of highlighting key features of the system and its successes and failures. This may prove useful in evaluating recent financial reforms.

Reform of the banking system or more generally the financial sector as a whole must be seen in the context of the entire economic reform "package" that China is attempting to implement. Financial reforms may depend crucially on certain other reforms; at the same time they may be prerequisites for the success of still other reforms elsewhere in the economy. Chapter 4 provides some general background information on overall economic reform policies and implementation in China since 1976, with special emphasis on how these interact with financial reforms. A chronological review of the implementation of financial reforms also is provided.

On the basis of the institutional discussion of Chapter 2 and the review of reform implementation in Chapter 4, the most important financial system reforms and policy changes are evaluated in Chapter 5. The crucial area of investment financing, however, is treated separately in Chapter 6. These two chapters contain the main analysis of recent reforms and policy changes. There is no need to repeat the conclusions stated there and in the final chapter, but not surprisingly it is found that results have been mixed. A certain degree of success has undoubtedly been attained, but certain pre-existing problems remain and new difficulties have emerged.

The centrally planned economies of Eastern Europe have to varying degrees been reforming their financial systems for over two decades. They have accumulated a wealth of experience which at least to some extent is relevant to China. The main "lessons" that can be distilled from the experience of Eastern European countries with financial reforms are outlined in Chapter 7. It is beyond the scope of this chapter to provide a detailed analysis; instead there are only brief comments.

Chapter 8 summarizes some of the main findings and conclusions of this study. Though any attempt to forecast the direction of future changes is fraught with uncertainty because the situation in China is still fluid, the main issues that are likely to continue to set the agenda for financial sector policies in the future will be briefly discussed. Since much of the quantitative information is utilized in more than one chapter, all of the tables are grouped after Chapter 8 for easy reference.

Finally, readers will note that most of this study is oriented toward the banking system and that in some respects the equally or perhaps more important fiscal system has been neglected. This was dictated to some extent by the need to limit the scope of the discussion in the interest of containing its length. It is also true that detailed published information on reforms and policy changes in the banking system became available to the author before materials of similar quality on the budget and fiscal policy. However, the most important reason for the focus on the banking system is that a major goal of economic reforms in China is to enhance the role of banks and the indirect policy instruments they use (interest rates and credit) in guiding economic activities. Banks are envisaged as at least to some extent replacing the directives of

command planning in influencing the decisions of micro-
level units. Thus as the direct control exercised by
the planning and administrative systems is weakened in
the process of economic reform, it is hoped that the
banking system will step in and, using much more
indirect mechanisms, help ensure that macroeconomic
objectives continue to be attained. In this light a
focus on the banking system is appropriate.

2
Institutional Framework

China's financial system as presently constituted includes nine national level organizations under two distinct administrative jurisdictions: the People's Bank of China (PBC) and the Ministry of Finance (MOF).[1] This institutional bifurcation has strongly influenced policies and reforms during the past several years; it underlies many of the problems and developments discussed in this monograph. The PBC is China's chief banking institution, an independent, ministry-level entity that reports directly to the State Council, the highest executive body in the Chinese government. The People's Insurance Company of China (PICC) has the status of a subordinate department of the PBC. The PBC also manages on behalf of the State Council three nominally independent organizations: the Bank of China (BOC), in charge of foreign exchange transactions, the General Administration of Foreign Exchange Control (GAFX), responsible for formulating and overseeing foreign exchange regulations, and the Agricultural Bank of China (ABC), which handles banking work in rural areas. The rural credit cooperatives, originally collective bodies ostensibly formed voluntarily by local peasants, are the grassroots units of the ABC.

On the fiscal side the Ministry of Finance (MOF) is the most important institution. It manages the People's Construction Bank of China (PCBC), which like the BOC, ABC, and GAFX is in theory subordinate only to the State Council itself. The PCBC handles state budget capital construction appropriations whether loans or grants, and in addition provides banking services to capital construction teams and various related units. The recently established China Investment Bank (CIB) will serve as a financial intermediary channelling funds from international

7

organizations like the World Bank to Chinese industrial
enterprises, to be used in modernization projects.
One other organization, the China International
Trust and Investment Corporation (CITIC), has a nominally high position directly below the State Council but
few real powers. Its main functions involve arranging
and facilitating joint ventures using Chinese and
foreign capital as well as handling investments in
China by foreign companies and overseas Chinese. All
joint ventures, however, must be approved by the
Foreign Investment Control Commission (FICC),[2] leaving
CITIC with little decisionmaking authority.
This relatively variegated organizational structure is only a few years old. During the Cultural
Revolution and its aftermath, the PBC was incorporated
in the MOF, and little was heard about or from it.
This amalgamation of fiscal and banking institutions,
involving the subordination of banking work to fiscal
goals, is now condemned as having been very harmful.
After the PBC was officially separated from the MOF, a
number of specialized financial institutions sprang up
or were restored to independent status. The BOC was
separated from the PBC in March 1979;[3] GAFX was
created at the same time, CITIC somewhat later in the
year.[4] There were several attempts to set up an
agricultural bank in the 1950s and 1960s, all short-
lived. The present incarnation of the ABC dates from
February 1979.[5] The PCBC was made an independent
entity directly under the State Council in August
1979.[6] The PICC resumed domestic insurance business
only at the beginning of 1980, after an interruption of
over 21 years.[7] Through most of the 1970s China's
banking system was under the control of the MOF, and
specialized banks either did not exist or were without
independent status.
The following sections look briefly at each of
China's main financial institutions, commenting on
their functions, organizational structure, role in
planning, relationship to other supervisory organs, and
quantitative significance. Some historical background
will also be provided.

THE PEOPLE'S BANK OF CHINA

The PBC is by far China's most comprehensive
banking institution, with an organizational network
permeating the entire economy. As an administrative
organ for government financial management and at the
same time an economic entity managing loan activities,
it has wide-ranging responsibilities. Despite some
departures, the PBC approaches fairly closely in formal
scope and authority the Soviet conception of the

"monobank", nerve center and monitor of the economy on both micro and macro levels.[8] It serves many of the functions that in market economies are the responsibility of the central bank, as well as performing services elsewhere handled by commercial banks, savings banks, and more recently, investment banks. The PBC is the country's center of cash, credit, and settlements transactions.[9] By virtue of its monopoly position it is supposedly able to monitor the degree of plan fulfillment, efficacy of financial management, and other activities of producers and other lower-level units in the economy.

The PBC is the only organization in China permitted to issue currency, and is responsible for devising and implementing national and regional plans for cash in circulation. The so-called cash plan, however, is largely determined by the credit plan and state budget, rather than independently formulated. With a few exceptions related to China's capital construction system and state farms, all state-owned enterprises and other government entities, as well as Party Committees and mass organizations, must keep their funds in an account at one and only one PBC branch. Only very small payments can be made in currency, using strictly limited cash reserves that units are allowed to keep in their possession. All other transactions in the state sector of the economy must be consummated by appropriate crediting and debiting of the parties' bank accounts. Thus the PBC is able to monitor and supervise the financial affairs of enterprises. Again with few exceptions, all loans of circulating funds (working capital) are supposed to emanate from the PBC. Interenterprise trade credit, either negotiable or involuntary, has been strictly forbidden in the past. This monopoly on credit in theory gives the PBC a powerful tool with which to influence the behavior of its clients, though in practice banks often have little ability to withhold loans. The PBC is also responsible for overall credit planning; credit plans of individual units, however, depend mainly on their output plans, and unplanned credit to finance inventory accumulation is common.

The PBC holds savings accounts of individuals in urban areas and sets interest rates on all loans and deposits, subject to approval by the State Council. Except for state-budgeted capital construction funds, it handles revenue accruing to and disbursements from the national treasury. Foreign exchange rates are set by the PBC, which has overall responsibility for international activities, though the BOC manages day-to-day transactions. Another important function of the PBC is supervision of disbursements from enterprise wage funds.

The PBC is also responsible for handling transactions in gold and other precious metals, setting purchase prices subject to State Council approval. Since March 1, 1980, banks have bought gold within China at Y 406.25 per liang (approximately US$203 per troy ounce), silver at 0.20 per gram (about US$4.15 per troy ounce), and platinum at Y 25 per gram (US$18.95 per troy ounce).[10] These represent increases of 328 percent, 100 percent and 174 percent respectively over previous purchase prices, which at least in the case of gold had remained unchanged since the 1950s.[11] Private ownership of precious metals is not illegal, but transactions between individuals in gold, silver, and foreign currencies are strictly prohibited.

In order to carry out its duties the PBC has a vast organizational network. As of the end of 1979 there were a total of over 15,000 different PBC subunits throughout the country, including 29 provincial-level branch banks, one for each province, autonomous region, and centrally-administered municipality, 148 municipal-level subbranches (in cities directly subordinate to the provinces), 220 central subbranches in prefectures, 2,777 county-level subbranch banks, and 2,883 offices under the jurisdiction of county-level subbranches. The PBC has a total of 330,000 employees,[12] including only 1,200 at the head office in Beijing.[13] The latter is divided into 14 departments including the headquarters of the PICC. In terms of location of personnel the PBC is highly decentralized. PBC branches are under the "dual leadership" of the head office and provincial Party Committees or revolutionary committees. In professional work the leadership of Beijing is supposed to be primary, while in the realm of political work and Party affairs the localities play the dominant role.[14]

In July 1981 the PBC for the first time published comprehensive statistics on money and credit, presented in Table 1. Since then similar banking statistics have been published in the journal Zhongguo Jinrong (China's Finance) on a quarterly basis. We can now gain some impression of the financial flows passing through the PBC and the specialized banks that it manages. The state sector (first four categories of deposits) accounted for 68.5 percent of total domestic deposits at the end of both 1980 and 1981, down only slightly from 1979. Within this group the biggest increase from 1979 to 1982 was in capital construction funds, probably reflecting cutbacks of actual expenditures in this sector. Urban savings deposits jumped nearly 40 percent in 1980 and over 25 percent in 1981, following an increase of 30.8 percent in 1979.[15] A further rise of nearly 21 percent occurred during the first three quarters of 1982,[16] followed by an increase of 4.5 percent

in the last quarter of the year. Other noteworthy
aspects on the sources of funds side are a 64 percent
rise in currency outstanding between 1979 and 1982 and
a 65 percent decline in the bank's surplus between 1979
and 1981, followed by a doubling in 1982.

On the credit side, the bulk of all loans
outstanding are for working capital as opposed to fixed
investment.[17] The most striking change, however, has
been the institution on a significant scale of loans by
the PBC for purchase of equipment, mainly directed to
China's light and textile industries. Loans to urban
collectives and individual businesses rose sharply in
1979-1982 as a result of increased government attention
to these sectors of the economy. Loans to state farms
also grew quickly, while working capital credit to the
urban state sector (first three categories) grew more
slowly and was progressively squeezed, increasing by
14.5 percent in 1980, 13.5 percent in 1981, and
6.9 percent in 1982.

In both 1979 and 1980 the PBC advanced large sums
to the MOF to cover unprecedented budget deficits. One
minor puzzle concerns the fact that China's 1980 realized budget deficit was Y 12.75 billion, Y 4.75 billion more than the original plan,[18] while only
Y 8 billion was turned over to the MOF by the PBC in
that year. Most likely the 1981 issue of Treasury
bonds was designed to absorb this difference. Since
government deficit spending is first reflected in a
rise in bank deposits of the recipients of appropriations, it was probably not necessary for the PBC to
advance more money in the short run. The PBC advances
to the treasury are not bonds; according to the
Minister of Finance an undisclosed rate of interest is
being charged.[19] Budget surpluses and deficits from
different years apparently can be set off against each
other freely.

We have some information on long-term growth rates
of financial aggregates in China. The figures in
Table 2 provide an indication of the general trends.
Monetary growth has been highly erratic. Moreover the
growth of currency, individual deposits, and enterprise
deposits has been even more variable than that of the
money supply as a whole. Growth rates of these main
components of the money stock show very little correla-
tion, except in the past several years. This suggests
that the factors determining different components of
the money supply do not necessarily work in the same
direction. The money supply grew at an average annual
rate of over 26 percent between 1978 and 1981. This
probably exceeded the growth warranted by the expansion
of economic activity during this period. Total outstanding loans of the state banking system grew at an

average annual rate of over 14 percent between 1978 and
1981, which also seems somewhat excessive.[20]
     The PBC at present enjoys a status in the Chinese
economic management system that it has rarely had since
the 1950s. The Maoist distaste for material incentives
was easily transformed into attacks on bank work and
financial accounting in general during mass political
campaigns like the Great Leap Forward and Cultural
Revolution. More insidiously, the desire for rapid
growth of production with attention focussed on heavy
industry and steel in particular tended to undermine
professional bank concerns about timely loan repayments, prompt settlement of accounts, and controlled
extension of new credit.
     Until recently, the PBC's internal structure was
highly centralized; local branches were forced to
follow in detail plans sent down from above. They had
little decisionmaking authority. At the same time,
local banks were subservient to Party and government
authorities in the areas where they were located. From
1958 until 1979 local Party or revolutionary committees
were in charge of appointment, dismissal, transfer, and
promotion of bank personnel in places under their
jurisdiction.[21] This meant that political criteria
often dominated the choice of bank cadres, specialized
training and even elementary financial accounting were
neglected, and bank employees in making specific loan
decisions were easily influenced by personal connec-
tions with those who had appointed them. Local Party
committees would often make direct requests for specific loan projects, which could not be refused.[22]
     Another manifestation of PBC weakness was the
periodically repeated phenomenon: "capital construction squeezes state finance, state finance squeezes the
banks, and the banks issue currency."[23] Excessive
fixed investment plans caused fiscal authorities to cut
back budgetary allocations of circulating capital in
order to maintain a balanced budget, which forced
enterprises to go to banks for loan funds with which to
stay in business. In this situation banks found it
extremely difficult to withhold credit, since doing so
might cause a client severe problems through no fault
of its own. Partly as a result, there has been a
long-term tendency for circulating capital loans to
rise relative to budgeted circulating capital allot-
ments and measures of output or income. The increase
in the relative importance of bank credit in providing
circulating capital was not until recently accompanied
by any strengthening of bank control over enterprise
financial affairs.
     The PBC was established on December 1, 1948, 11
months before the People's Republic of China itself
came into existence.[24] During the 1950s and 1960s it

was a ministry-level institution reporting directly to the highest government executive organ – first the General Administrative Council, then after 1954 the State Council. The private banking sector was nationalized and incorporated into the state system relatively early. This process was essentially completed when the Joint State-Private Bank, an amalgamation of remaining privately-owned banks, became a de facto agent of the PBC in 1953.[25] According to another source this takeover was formally consummated only in 1955.[26] In this period the PBC played a major role in controlling the hyperinflation inherited by the new regime in 1949 and in furthering the socialization of industry, commerce, and later agriculture. These successes brought it considerable prestige.

This was soon dissipated as the focus of bank work shifted to supervision and monitoring of state-owned enterprises. Restrictive policies and attempts by the PBC to promote more careful financial accounting by enterprises during the First Five Year Plan period (1953-1957) achieved only incomplete success. A major weakening of the PBC occurred in 1958 during the Great Leap Forward, when local bank branches came under the domination of their localities' Party Committees. At the height of the Great Leap Forward all bank work was oriented toward expanding local production, especially in the backyard iron and steel furnace campaign. Previously established banking principles were ignored, and all possible means were used to raise funds for local iron and steel production using indigenous technology. The output produced turned out to be adulterated and unusable in modern production or finishing processes. Even more serious, the massive diversion of resources from agriculture combined with several bad harvests in a row threatened subsistence levels of living in China's countryside. In the subsequent readjustment period the banking system was strengthened and at least partly recentralized.

According to one western source the PBC as an organization survived the Cultural Revolution (1966-1968) relatively unscathed.[27] But more damaging was its long aftermath, during which the PBC was made a subordinate part of the MOF. This exacerbated the problem of fiscal objectives taking priority while banking activities were relegated to a secondary position. The PBC regained its independent status only after the fall of the "Gang of Four" in 1976. Since then it has been trying to repair past damage and expand its role as a flexible expediter of economic development.

THE AGRICULTURAL BANK OF CHINA AND RURAL CREDIT COOPERATIVES

The ABC is a specialized institution in charge of rural banking. According to the State Council circular that ordered its restoration, the ABC is responsible for unified management of all state financial appropriations for the rural economy, with the exception of state-budgeted capital construction in agriculture, forestry and hydroelectricity, which continues to be handled by the PCBC.[28] Though the ABC nominally answers directly to the State Council, the PBC is charged with managing it on behalf of the latter. Each ABC branch is supposed to forward its credit and cash plans to the corresponding PBC branch at the same level, so that they can be included in the aggregate state credit and cash plans. Other than this the exact mode of supervision by the PBC is left unspecified. More recently the ABC and other specialized banks were required to "report monthly to the local people's banks on the progress of credit plans and the conditions of cash flow."[29]

All ABC branches from the provincial level on down are independent accounting units, which means they calculate their own profits and losses. As profit-oriented units they are supposed to receive a commission or fee for handling government financial appropriations to support agriculture. The ABC should not be responsible for paying subsidies involved in special low interest or interest-free loans made in accordance with state policy. Interbranch relationships among ABC units at all levels and between ABC units and PBC branches have the characteristics of dealings between independent accounting units, with interest calculated and paid on interbank deposits. Each ABC branch is under the "dual leadership" of the head office and the local revolutionary committee. In professional bank work direction comes from the head office, while in Party work and political affairs the guidance of local authorities is primary. Personnel decisions are supposed to be handled internally by the ABC. In these respects the ABC's organization parallels that of the PBC.

All deposits and loans of state offices in the countryside, rural mass organizations, schools, state farms, etc., are handled by the ABC, which also supervises their cash management and noncash transactions. Rural collectives, including communes, brigades, teams, and supply and marketing cooperatives, individual commune members, and commune and brigade-run enterprises, have their deposits and loans managed by the rural credit cooperatives. Though these latter organizations are encouraged to keep their funds in the credit cooperatives, they are not required to do so. The ABC is also supposed to provide rural collectives with guidance on financial accounting and managing funds.

While the present version of the ABC is only a little more than two years old, its grassroots units, the rural credit cooperatives, have formed a relatively complete rural financial network since the late 1950s. Their position was strengthened and secured by the same directive that reestablished the ABC. The credit cooperatives as their name implies are nominally collective institutions formed voluntarily by the peasants. The general pattern is for each commune or in some cases each brigade to have a credit cooperative, with subordinate credit service stations and credit cooperative members' small groups at the brigade and production team levels respectively.[30] This was the situation in the mid-1960s, when there were at least 100,000 rural credit cooperatives in China.[31] Recent statements giving figures ranging from 62,000 to 70,000 for the total number of credit cooperatives suggest that some consolidation has occurred over the years.[32] Since China has upwards of 50,000 people's communes, the predominant pattern at present must be one credit cooperative in each commune. The February 1979 State Council circular that restored the ABC urged that salaries and benefits of employees of the credit cooperatives be raised to the uniform standards for ABC workers. This suggests that in the past they may have been poorly rewarded. The directive also prohibits indiscriminate transfer or diversion of credit cooperative funds by other units, a sign that this may have been a common phenomenon in the past.

Building the organizational network of the ABC has taken a considerable length of time. The ABC now has provincial, prefectural, and county branch offices as well as business offices in some people's communes. These business offices were previously part of the PBC network and like the credit cooperatives were simply transferred to ABC jurisdiction. Though changes at the lower levels must have been fairly straightforward, setting up the superstructure was more difficult. In many parts of the country the ABC's organizational infrastructure was not in place until 1980.[33] As of early in that year the ABC had opened 26 provincial-level branches, 160 prefectural central subbranches, and 1,150 county-level subbranches. Total employment was then over 230,000. The collective rural banking network included 62,000 credit cooperatives with a total of 260,000 workers and 356,000 credit offices in production brigades, with nearly 400,000 part-time operatives.[34] A different source states that the ABC has 27,000 branches (presumably including commune credit offices) with a total of 230,000 employees, as well as 59,000 credit cooperatives with 260,000 employees and 350,000 brigade credit offices with 360,000 part-time workers.[35] Either way, China has a rural banking network of over 400,000 units with a total of between 850,000 and 900,000 full-time and part-time staff, dwarfing the PBC in these respects. The ABC probably has grown somewhat since early 1980 as the rest of rural China has been included in its scope of operations.

Table 3 presents official data on the aggregate loans and deposits of rural credit cooperatives. Deposits far exceed loans: the latter only amounted to 22 percent of the former at the end of 1979, 30 percent at the end of 1980 and 1981. Most of the difference is presumably deposited with the ABC, which then has more resources with which to make rural loans. The large gap between deposits and loans strongly suggests that the credit cooperatives' nominally independent status does not mean much in terms of actual operations. Otherwise each credit cooperative might prefer to use all of its deposits for local loans to its own members. Among deposits at rural credit cooperatives, those of individual commune members have shown rapid steady increases since 1976, growing at an average annual rate of nearly 35 percent between 1976 and 1982 (Table 12). "Other" deposits dropped sharply in 1981, perhaps reflecting reductions in balances held at certain credit cooperatives by the ABC. Loans to individual commune members increased rapidly in 1980-1982, largely as a result of the implementation of rural economic reforms. The stagnation in loans outstanding to rural collectives in 1981 and 1982 reflects the implementa- tion of the rural production responsibility system, which decreased the economic role of collectives and enhanced that of small groups and individuals.

We can compare current statistics on rural credit cooperatives with figures for 1957. At the end of that year deposits in the 88,368 credit cooperatives totalled Y 2,065.8 million and loans outstanding Y 565.8 million.[36] The ratio of loans to deposits (27.4 percent) is roughly comparable to that in 1979-1981. Total deposits increased at an average annual rate of 12.1 percent from 1957 to 1981, while the average annual growth rate of loans during the same period was 12.5 percent. These high long-term growth rates mask substantial ups and downs, some of which are apparent from the data on individual deposits in Table 12.

China's published banking statistics provide no separate information on the ABC. The consolidated data presented in Table 1, however, does permit certain observations. Loans for advance payments, to communes

and brigades, and to state farms are made by the ABC.
At the end of 1980 these totalled Y 17,588 million, an
increase of Y 3,914 million or 28.6 percent compared
with the balance outstanding at the end of 1979. In
1981 there was a rise of Y 1,667 million or 9.5 percent, and in 1982 a further increase of Y 1,990 million
or 10.3 percent. Deposits in rural areas grew by
Y 3,613 million or 17.7 percent in 1980, by Y 3,856
million or 16.1 percent in 1981, and by Y 5,154 million
or 18.5 percent in 1982. According to this data, the
ABC's deposits exceeded loans by Y 6,697 million at the
end of 1979, Y 6,396 million at the end of 1980,
Y 8,585 million at the end of 1981, and Y 11,749 million at the end of 1982.

The total value of deposits in rural areas net of
interbranch balances within the banking system cannot
be estimated without making an assumption about the
proportions of the excess of credit cooperative
deposits over loans held in cash and in accounts at ABC
branches. The lowest estimate of total rural deposits
results from assuming that the entire difference
between credit cooperative deposits and loans is deposited with the ABC in the category of "deposits in rural
areas." In this case total rural deposits are the sum
of deposits at the ABC ("deposits in rural areas") and
loans outstanding from RCCs. Based on these calculations, total rural deposits were Y 25,125 million at
the end of 1979, Y 32,148 million at the end of 1980,
Y 37,478 million at the end of 1981, and Y 45,109
million at the end of 1982. Total loans outstanding
(adding those of the ABC to those of the credit
cooperatives) were Y 18,428 million at the end of 1979,
Y 25,752 million at the end of 1980, Y 28,893 million
at the end of 1981, and Y33,360 million at the end of
1982. Rural deposits thus exceed rural loans by a wide
margin even under the most conservative assumptions.

Aside from an inactive and short-lived
Agricultural Cooperative Bank that was formed in July
1951, there were two previous attempts to set up an
agricultural bank in China, one in 1955 and one in
1963. The first attempt was terminated and the ABC
abolished in April 1957.[37] The second agricultural
bank lasted until October 1965, but no details are
available on the reasons for its demise.[38] In 1957,
the ABC was felt to duplicate functions performed by
the PBC, leading to wasteful overhead and and problems
of coordination. The completion of a certain degree of
collectivization in the rural economy provided a new
channel for transforming savings into investment (by
means of accumulation by the collectives themselves),
making the need for an agricultural bank seem less
urgent. Finally, the ABC was associated with the
semi-coercive methods of obtaining savings deposits,

the overly rapid expansion of loans, and the neglect of
loan repayments that characterized the process of rural
collectivization and the establishment of the credit
cooperatives themselves.[39] Today conditions seem
sufficiently changed that factors militating against
the success and viability of the ABC in the past are no
longer important. The proliferation of various kinds
of grants and loans supporting agriculture makes the
need for unified management by a specialized agricultural bank even greater than it was in the past. The
rural credit cooperatives have never had their existence threatened, though at the height of the Great Leap
Forward there was some consideration of merging them
with the people's communes. But lack of independence
has been the rule for them, both in relation to local
Party and collective organizations and internally in
dealing with the PBC or ABC.[40]

China's rural banking system faces many important
tasks at present. One major objective is to institute
unified management of funds for agricultural investment
to ensure that high returns are achieved, duplication
and waste avoided. In discussing past performance one
scholar comments:

> The agricultural aid funds are allocated evenly
> without focal points, so that the due effects
> have not been achieved... In some localities
> substantial portions of these funds have been
> embezzled and not put to use in the communes or
> production brigades.[41]

Given the multitude of appropriations and
subsidies from different sources and the entrenched
vested interests of those who have controlled these
funds in the past, unified management will be no easy
job. Nevertheless, progress is being made toward this
objective in at least some areas. For instance, in
the Xinjiang Autonomous Region, ABC branches supervise
the allocation of 82 percent of all fiscal appropriations in support of agriculture.[42] Another vital
objective is to instill accurate financial accounting
methods in rural collectives. Finally and perhaps most
important, the ABC as well as the rural credit cooperatives must adjust to and support the production
responsibility system and other reforms in rural areas.

THE BANK OF CHINA AND OTHER ORGANS
INVOLVED IN INTERNATIONAL WORK

The BOC is China's specialized foreign exchange
bank. According to its new charter, published in

September 1980, it is authorized to engage in the
following international business activities:

(1) International account settling for foreign
trade and nontrade transactions.
(2) Credit relations with international banks.
(3) Overseas Chinese remittances and other
international remittances.
(4) Foreign currency deposits and loans as well
as foreign exchange business in accordance
with savings and loan practices permitted by
the People's Bank of China.
(5) Foreign exchange transactions.
(6) International gold transactions.
(7) Organization or participation in
international consortium loans.
(8) Investment in or joint operation of banks,
financial corporations, or other enterprises
in the Hong Kong-Macao area and in foreign
countries.
(9) Issuance of foreign currency bonds and other
negotiable securities, in accordance with
the power delegated by the state.
(10) Crediting and consulting.
(11) Other bank activities permitted or
commissioned by the state.[43]

The BOC was made directly subordinate to the State
Council in March 1979.[44] In practice, however, it has
little authority to make major decisions, handling
day-to-day transactions with little direct voice in
making policy.
Internally, all foreign exchange holdings of
Chinese organizations and individuals must be deposited
with the BOC. All foreign exchange transactions must
be made through the BOC.[45] In practice these theoretically strict regulations are sometimes bypassed. For
example, numerous Chinese enterprises in Guangdong
Province until recently had been putting away considerable amounts of foreign exchange in foreign bank
accounts. Despite a crackdown on these activities,
120 firms convinced the authorities that their deposits
abroad are necessary for their conduct of business and
therefore were allowed to keep a total of US$ 45.6 mil-
lion in various overseas accounts.[46] The Chinese
banking system's ability to monitor and control foreign
exchange transactions appears to have decreased
somewhat as a result of reforms that allow localities
and even some enterprises to retain a portion of their
foreign exchange earnings. While official foreign
exchange rates fluctuate between Y 1.5 and Y 2 to US$1,
in internal calculations a rate of Y 2.8 to US$1 has
been used since the beginning of 1981. Subsidies which

previously had been paid on export products were supposed to be eliminated at the same time.[47] Apparently
enterprises can sometimes trade their foreign exchange
holdings at even higher rates, reportedly as high as Y
3.36 to the dollar.[48]

The BOC had seventy-seven domestic branches as
of July 1980, one for each province, autonomous region,
and centrally-administered municipality, the rest
concentrated in localities with large amounts of
foreign trade.[49] Aside from handling foreign exchange
transactions and accounts, the BOC's most important
domestic activity is making foreign currency loans to
Chinese enterprises, primarily for export-oriented
projects in the light and textile industries. Recently
the procedures for foreign currency loans were
streamlined and a floating interest rate was adopted,
based on international market conditions. Perhaps more
important:

> The new regulations have also abandoned the
> previous practice of only giving loans to
> enterprises that produce goods for export.
> The scope of loans has been expanded to cover
> units which can earn foreign exchange directly
> or indirectly.[50]

In order to increase flexibility, the BOC now can
extend loans in domestic currency to finance Chinese-
manufactured equipment needed for projects supported by
foreign exchange loans. Some export enterprises have
domestic currency accounts with the BOC to facilitate
transactions.[51] At least one BOC branch has offered
foreign exchange savings accounts to overseas Chinese
and residents of Hong Kong and Macao; they carry annual
interest rates of between 8.5 percent and 11.5 percent
for fixed-term time deposits.[52] It is not known
exactly what interest rates are paid on foreign
currency accounts of domestic residents and Chinese
organizations. Undoubtedly they are much lower, and
certain types of accounts pay no interest at all.[53]

China owns a considerable part of Hong Kong's
banking system. According to one source 12 of Hong
Kong's 75 licensed banks were owned by China, accounting in the early 1970s for 17 percent of Hong Kong's
total bank deposits and 10 percent of total lending.[54] BOC Hong Kong branches are in overall charge
of Chinese-owned and Chinese-affiliated banks in the
colony. Banking operations in Hong Kong are a source
of foreign currency for the PRC, in addition to facilitating foreign trade flows. Recently, more detailed
information has been provided about 8 BOC-affiliated
commercial banks with offices in Hong Kong (and one in

Singapore). Their total capital is Y 2.3 billion and
they have a total of 133 branches.[55]
     The BOC regularly publishes data on its assets and
liabilities (it is required to do so by the governments
of certain foreign countries in which it has established branch offices). This information for the years
1977-1979 is presented in Table 4. The BOC's capital
was substantially increased to Y 400 million in 1975
and remained fixed at that level until 1979. The new
BOC charter of September 1980 lists its capital as
Y 1 billion: the increase to this amount may have
occurred somewhat earlier. Quantitative information on
the BOC's domestic banking activities is more scanty.
In 1979 and 1980 it lent a total of US$9.1 billion in
foreign exchange to various Chinese entities (of which
$6.3 billion was repaid by the end of 1980). By the
end of 1981 the total value of all BOC domestic
currency loans outstanding reached Y 37.1 billion, up
84 percent compared with 1978.[56]
     China's attitude toward foreign indebtedness has
undergone several changes over the years. The country
incurred massive debt obligations to the USSR during
the 1950s, which were repaid after the Sino-Soviet
rift. During the late 1960s complete avoidance of
foreign indebtedness was China's goal; this resulted in
many restrictions on the types of activities the BOC
could become involved in. Since the early 1970s this
policy has gradually changed, and at present the BOC
can make nearly any kind of internationally acceptable
transaction, including those that are accompanied by
foreign debts of varying size and duration. China also
has borrowed more heavily than at any time since the
1950s. Nevertheless, the retrenchment of 1981, including cancellation of some important foreign-financed
projects, shows that China will continue to avoid the
large debts and debt service problems characteristic of
certain Eastern European countries in 1970s, even at
some cost in economic growth. Recently released
figures on China's gold and foreign exchange reserves
confirm this assessment. At the end of 1980 the
country had US$2,262 million in foreign exchange and
12.8 million troy ounces of gold (worth US$5,120
million at $400 per ounce). By the end of 1981 foreign
exchange reserves had jumped to $4,773 million, while
gold reserves had fallen slightly to 12.67 million troy
ounces. At the end of the third quarter of 1982
foreign exchange reserves reached $9,228 million and
gold reserves remained constant,[57] while by the end
of the year foreign exchange reserves had further grown
to US$11,125 million. One source estimated that as of
the end of 1980 China's total foreign indebtedness
would be US$3.4 billion.[58] This adds up to a very low

ratio of debt to reserves, though actual debt may have
turned out to be higher than predicted and the
$3.4 billion figure may not include delayed payment
obligations or various forms of short-term indebtedness. The current policy is to limit annual debt
repayment requirements (interest and principal) to less
than 20% of hard-currency exports.[59]
   In the past two or more years China has emphasized
obtaining concessional loan terms from foreign governments and international organizations, and utilizing
"new" types of foreign trade that avoid debt financing.
These include joint ventures, compensation trade,
cooperative production, processing and assembly of
imported materials, and countertrade. These methods of
obtaining foreign financing for investment will be
considered in Chapter 6.
   The BOC was founded in 1908, making it the oldest
Chinese banking institution still functioning.[60]
Before 1949 it concentrated on international banking
activities and established numerous branches in foreign
countries. Both before and after that date it was a
joint public-private bank with two-thirds of its
capital belonging to the Chinese government and one-
third to individual investors. This status was
officially changed only by the 1980 charter, which
states that "The Bank of China is a socialistic,
state-operated enterprise, and acts as the state's
special foreign exchange bank."[61] All increases in
the BOC's capital presumably have been appropriated by
the government, and there is no evidence that private
shareholders had any significant influence on BOC
operations after 1949. From early 1950 on, when Nan
Hanchen, then Director of the PBC, became Chairman of
the Board of the BOC, the latter became for all
practical purposes a subsidiary of the former.[62] It
is doubtful whether the 1979 change in its nominal
status has significantly enhanced the BOC's true
position within the banking system. But the BOC now
has more prestige, which may be useful in international
negotiations.
   The General Administration of Foreign Exchange
Control (GAFX) was established in March 1979 by the
same State Council circular that changed the status of
the BOC. The GAFX has the same nominal position as the
BOC (directly subordinate to the State Council), and the
president of the BOC concurrently serves as director of
the GAFX. Its functions include formulating laws and
regulations on foreign exchange, verifying and supervising foreign exchange receipts and disbursements,
periodically announcing foreign exchange rates, and
ensuring an overall balance of payments.[63] This last
responsibility suggests that the GAFX may have some

role in foreign exchange planning. Alternatively, it may have been set up to provide an independent check to prevent serious balance of payments problems from arising. This kind of mechanism has become all the more necessary as foreign exchange retention at various levels is now permitted. The main accomplishment of the GAFX so far has been the formulation of the "Provisional Regulations for Exchange Control in the People's Republic of China," promulgated by the State Council on December 18, 1980 and effective March 1, 1981.[64]

The China International Trust and Investment Corporation (CITIC) was established by State Council decree on July 8, 1979.[65] It is directly subordinate to the State Council and is not officially supervised by any other organization. According to its general manager, Rong Yiren, CITIC is

> "a business enterprise charged with promoting foreign investment in China... [It] will work with foreign investors in finding business opportunities for them in China, putting them in touch with potential Chinese partners, assisting them in negotiating the terms of a joint venture, and maintaining a friendly interest in their success. [It] will also find suitable foreign partners on the request of our national enterprises.[66]

CITIC does not have the authority to give final approval to joint venture contracts already negotiated and signed by the parties themselves. That is the responsibility of the Foreign Investment Control Commission.[67] In essence CITIC is an intermediary arranging contacts between potential Chinese and foreign joint venture partners. It does have a capital of Y 200 million, however, and is allowed to make investments in China on behalf of foreign individuals and firms.[68] CITIC's charter gives it responsibility for floating foreign currency-denominated bonds, but nothing has yet materialized on this score. As of mid-1981 negotiations were underway with Japanese financial institutions.[69]

Numerous provinces have also set up internationally-oriented trust corporations which appear to have no ties with CITIC. The Fujian Investment Enterprise Company has already issued long-term bonds denominated in domestic currency, which are being purchased mainly by Hong Kong residents and overseas Chinese.[70] Yen-denominated bonds for the Japanese market to finance construction of sugar refineries in Fujian were a possibility in 1981.[71] Clearly CITIC is

only one among several actors in this field and
probably not the most important one.

THE PEOPLE'S INSURANCE COMPANY OF CHINA

China had no domestic insurance between 1958 and
1979.[72] International insurance business was also
disrupted temporarily after the Cultural Revolution.[73]
Theoretically there is no need for domestic insurance
in the state sector of the economy, since property
owned by the government can be replaced with government
appropriations. This and the idea that insurance
premia constituted a "financial drag" on enterprises
were the main justifications for dismantling the
domestic insurance system. In actual practice,
however, it has proved impossible for the state to make
timely and complete restitutions for losses. Budgetary
processes take time, and given a shortage of funds the
government might decide not to replace losses in
certain enterprises or industries. Neither the state
nor any other organizations maintained reserve funds
against accidents and natural disasters, though some
reserves of strategic materials were provided for in
the plan. By contrast, an insurance system makes
planning and forecasting much easier for lower-level
units. Small, steady expenditures can be substituted
for large, unpredictable ones. Moreover, the reserve
funds of the insurance company are another source of
accumulation for the state.[74]
    The People's Insurance Company of China (PICC) at
present is directly subordinate to the PBC, though in
the 1950s it was under the supervision of the Ministry
of Finance.[75] It was founded on October 20, 1949, and
in 1951 its business received a great boost when
insurance was made compulsory for state enterprises and
various other units.[76] The PICC supervises two joint
state-private insurance companies, the Insurance
Company of China and the Taiping Insurance Company,
whose activities are limited to Hong Kong, Macao, and
Singapore.[77]
    In the past few years China has rapidly expanded
its international insurance activities. The PICC's
1979 international accounts are presented in Table 5.
Global direct business income from insurance premia in
that year came to Y 171.2 million, compared with just
over Y 137 million in 1978.[78] China's indemnity rate
is variously reported at 50-67 percent, while for
insurance on goods exported to Hong Kong and Macao it
is only 7-10 percent.[79] This makes China's international insurance business a very profitable earner of
foreign exchange.

The idea of gradually restoring China's domestic insurance system was broached publicly at a February 1979 national conference of PBC provincial-level branch directors. A meeting to discuss insurance work held in November 1979 decided to reinstate domestic business on an experimental basis in 1980, concentrating on the three cities of Beijing, Tianjin, and Shanghai. In addition, each province and autonomous region could designate three to five cities where insurance work would proceed. First priority was given to reinstituting property insurance for state enterprises, transportation insurance for goods, and household property insurance.[80] In contrast to the situation in the 1950s, insurance coverage was to be voluntary even for state-owned units. The only major exception is compulsory insurance for passengers on trains, ships, and airplanes.[81]

By the end of 1980 the PICC had reopened over 160 domestic branches all over China.[82] The total value of domestic insurance coverage reached over Y 144 billion at the end of 1980, Y 256 billion by the end of 1982.[83] The PICC strives to provide prompt payment for all valid claims so as to minimize disruption of production. In addition to property and transportation insurance, vehicle and third party liability coverage are now being offered.[84] The PICC is charged with playing a constructive role in economic readjustment:

> For those enterprises which will close, merge or retool during the readjustment, the corporation ⌊PICC⌋ will assist in management and transfer of property to minimize loss and damage. We will also streamline cancellation if any wish to withdraw coverage.[85]

From the viewpoint of investment financing the PICC is of only marginal significance. Since it is supposed to deposit its reserve funds with the PBC rather than investing them itself it cannot be considered a true financial intermediary. According to one report, however, the Tianjin PICC branch can deposit a portion of its funds with the local trust corporation, which in turn would use the money to make investments.[86]

THE MINISTRY OF FINANCE

The MOF is China's national fiscal institution. As such it has the task of compiling the central government's annual budgets and long-term financial plans. The MOF collects government revenues and makes budgetary disbursements, But all its funds are kept in

treasury accounts at the PBC. The MOF supervises the
financial work of other ministries and state organs as
well as the operations of finance and taxation departments.[87] It also reviews and
approves local government budgets before they are
submitted to the State Council and then the various
People's Congresses for final ratification.[88] Among
the other duties of the MOF are formulating tax and
budget regulations and overseeing interprovincial
fiscal transfers.

In the past the MOF had a strong influence over
China's banks. As mentioned before, during the early
and mid-1970s it had direct supervisory authority over
the PBC. Even now it is responsible for managing the
PCBC. The relationship between China's state financial
administration and the banking system is very close,
but at the same time it is inevitably subject to a
certain amount of friction. There are numerous areas
where jurisdictions and activities overlap. Working
capital funds for state enterprises are provided partly
by means of budget appropriations in the form of
nonrepayable grants, partly by PBC bank loans. In many
respects these are substitutes from the viewpoint of
recipients. Short- and medium-term PBC loans for
equipment similarly are close substitutes for "tapping
potential" and renovation appropriations in the state
budget. Furthermore, many budgetary capital construction projects are now being funded by PCBC loans rather
than grants. The state budget includes appropriations
for the PBC, called "bank credit funds." The cash plan,
credit plan, and state budget are closely interrelated
and partially determined by each other. All in all,
the MOF and PBC must closely coordinate their activities. However, certain jurisdictional conflicts
between them remain unresolved. Among the most important are those concerning jurisdiction over loans for
investment, working capital financing, and procedures
required for obtaining foreign currency loans.
Division of responsibilities is sometimes based on
bureaucratic compromises that weaken coordination or
result in duplication.

China's revenues and expenditures by major category appear in Tables 6 and 7. A detailed examination
of this data and China's budget system is beyond the
scope of this study, but we will look at the role of
the budget in financing investment later (Chapter 6).
The unprecedented budget deficit of over Y 17 billion
in 1979 was financed partly by drawing on accumulated
budget surpluses from previous years, totalling about
Y 9 billion. An overdraft with the PBC covered the
rest.[89] The 1980 realized budget deficit of Y 12.75
billion was financed by an additional loan from the PBC

and Treasury bond issues, since accumulated past budget surpluses had been depleted. Six factors have been cited as contributing to the 1979 budget deficit:

(1) An increase in state purchase prices for farm and sideline products along with reductions in or exemptions from various rural taxes.
(2) Great efforts to increase employment in urban areas and wage increases for many workers.
(3) Increased retention of funds by enterprises and local authorities.
(4) Larger fiscal appropriations to develop agriculture and light industry.
(5) Increased defense spending.
(6) Back pay and other subsidies for rehabilitated victims of the Cultural Revolution.[90]

These forces undoubtedly continued to operate in 1980, except for (5). In 1981 the central government took drastic steps to reduce the budget deficit, the most important of which was a sharp 21 percent cutback in budgetary appropriations for capital construction investment. In 1982, despite a modest increase in revenues and expenditures overall, capital construction appropriations were apparently further reduced slightly. They are expected to increase significantly in 1983.

Over the long term the MOF has enjoyed the most stable position among China's financial institutions. It was established on October 20, 1949,[91] and since then has undergone no significant changes in its nominal status in the hierarchy. The degree of centralization in China's fiscal management, however, has been a subject of controversy and scholarly attention.[92]

China's national budget includes the budgetary revenues and expenditures of the provinces, which in turn include those of prefectures and municipalities, and so on down to the county level.[93] But local governments at all levels as well as enterprises receive revenues and make expenditures outside the budget; during most of the history of the PRC these so-called extrabudgetary funds were the main means by which local authorities could exercise their initiative and engage in activities without the prior approval of the central government. Most extrabudgetary funds are used for capital investments. One source calculated that extrabudgetary funds accounted for 55 percent of gross fixed investment in China's state-owned enterprises in 1980, compared with 40 percent in 1979,

38 percent in 1976, and only 11 percent during the
First Five Year Plan period. The same article went on
to list the main sources of extrabudgetary funds: (1)
funds raised by local authorities; (2) funds held by
economic departments; (3) the cash surplus from
operating expenses of administrative units; and (4)
funds diverted from other uses.[94] Extrabudgetary
funds were the main reason for China's failure to
control the aggregate level of investment in 1980. By
1981, extrabudgetary revenues reportedly totalled
Y 47 billion, nearly half as great as domestic
budgetary revenues.[95] Extrabudgetary funds as a
source of investment financing will be discussed in
more detail in Chapter 6.

THE PEOPLE'S CONSTRUCTION BANK OF CHINA

The PCBC is mainly a conduit for capital construction funds appropriated in China's state budget.
Funds raised by localities and enterprises for capital
construction are also supposed to be deposited at the
PCBC. The latter also acts as a true bank in making
(circulating capital and equipment) loans to and
handling the deposits of specialized construction and
installation enterprises, geological prospecting units,
and enterprises which supply construction materials.[96]
The PCBC handles settling of accounts in China's
capital construction system.[97] To carry out these
functions it has 2,700 branches throughout China, and a
total of 46,000 employees.[98] In November 1979 the
PCBC was made an independent organization directly
subordinate to the State Council, managed on its behalf
by the MOF and to a lesser extent the State Capital
Construction Commission.[99]
The PCBC is in charge of the transformation of
state capital construction appropriations from nonrepayable grants into interest-bearing loans. It
handles all such loans, which at present can be made
only to "independent accounting units" - mainly enterprises. Investment expenditures in the so-called
"nonproductive" sector - government, administration,
defense, scientific research, culture, education, and
public health - will continue to be grants disbursed by
the MOF.[100] Since interest rates on capital construction loans are low, the main effect on enterprise
decisionmaking will come from the fact that investment
expenditures are now repayable with the proceeds of the
projects concerned. This contrasts sharply with the
past, when investment funds were viewed as free gifts
for which units vigorously competed. Once funding was
obtained there was little reason for them to economize

in its utilization. Assuming profit maximizing
behavior, enterprises in the past had an incentive to
request funding for investment projects with large
negative rates of return. Perhaps they now will be
willing to undertake only those projects which earn at
least a small positive rate of return. Capital construction loans were first introduced on an experimental basis in eight enterprises in August 1979. In 1980
the PCBC granted capital construction loans for
budgeted capital construction projects totalling Y 1.4
billion; in 1981 the figure was Y 2.5 billion. In the
latter year, the PCBC also granted Y 2.48 billion in
capital construction loans which were financed by
deposits at the PCBC.[101]

The PCBC began operations in October 1954, taking
over functions that had been previously handled by the
Bank of Communications, a joint state-private institution with a long history going back to the late Qing
period.[102] As part of the decentralization measures
of 1958 the PCBC head office was absorbed by the MOF
and local branches put under the control of local
government authorities.[103] It regained some independence in the early 1960s; at that time an innovative
program involving small loans for technological
improvements was started in Shanghai.[104] In 1975 this
activity was put on a nationwide basis.[105] At the
same time the PCBC started granting special loans to
export enterprises all over China, based on a Shanghai
pilot program begun in 1972.[106] Though they were
relatively small in magnitude and still highly fiscal
in character, these loan programs did set a precedent
for financing investment by means of credit rather than
budgetary grants. The recent institution of capital
construction loans most likely has enhanced the PCBC's
decisionmaking role, since it now has greater authority
to approve or reject loan applications.

3
Policy and Performance, 1949–1976

BASIC PRINCIPLES OF BANKING IN A COMMAND ECONOMY

The role envisioned for the banking system in the classic Stalinian model of a centrally planned social- ist economy is relatively simple.[1] Correspondingly, its institutional structure is highly centralized and controlled by a single organization, the all-encompass- ing State Bank, commonly referred to as the "monobank." It is the sole institution allowed to issue currency, the only source of short-term credit in the economy, and the center through which all significant financial transactions in the state sector must pass. All state enterprises must keep an account at one and only one bank branch, and all their funds must be deposited in the bank, except for strictly limited cash reserves.[2] All state-sector transactions above a stipulated size must be made by means of appropriate crediting and debiting of the transactors' accounts (so-called "noncash settlement"). The State Bank is thus in a position to monitor the micro-level activities of the economy on an almost daily basis, something no other organization has the ability to do.

Bank supervision has two main objectives. One is plan fulfillment in the broadest sense. Banks must ensure that all activities of enterprises are consis- tent with and promote achievement of plan targets. They also should investigate any discrepancies that appear, which might provide advance warning of a unit's inability to fulfill its plan, and if possible take effective remedial action, or at least notify authori- ties in a position to do so. The two functions of passive monitoring and active correction of the plan can conflict if the plan is internally inconsistent, as it invariably is. The second goal is more vague: banks should encourage enterprises to improve their financial

31

management and maintain sound financial discipline.[3]
In practice achievement of the financial targets in an
enterprise's plan and timely repayment of debts are
taken as the main indicators of sound financial
management.

The most important sanction available to banks
in dealing with their clients in the state sector is
withholding of credit. Given the legal prohibition
against transferable or nontransferable interenterprise trade credit, the banks theoretically can
strongly influence the scale of a firm's operations by
changing the amount of short-term credit it grants. In
principle bank credit is supposed to cover only the
seasonal and unexpected temporary working capital
requirements of enterprises; nonrepayable budgetary
grants are used for both fixed investment and normal
year-round working capital needs. In actual practice,
however, measures have been taken to make sure that all
state-owned enterprises require some short-term bank
credit in order to maintain business operations at the
planned level. In the USSR "quota" allowances of
working capital to be provided as grants from the
government budget were arbitrarily set low enough that
all enterprises, even those without periodic variations
in scale of operations, required some additional bank
credit.[4] In China in the early 1960s 20 percent of an
enterprise's quota of working capital was supposed to
be supplied by bank loans, as well as all above-quota
needs.[5] Regardless of the method used, close bank
involvement with the entire state sector by means of
credit relations is assured.

Credit is granted according to five basic principles: (1) it is planned, (2) it must be used for a
specific purpose, (3) it is secured by physical
resources in the possession of the borrower, generally
inventories, (4) it is repayable, and (5) it has a
fixed maturity.[6] Of these criteria, (1) is the least
adhered to in practice; unplanned loans are made
willingly if refusal to do so would make achievement of
physical plan targets more difficult. No attempt is
made to influence an enterprise's decision whether or
not to ask for credit by changing the terms on which it
is offered. In other words, interest rates are not
used to adjust either the aggregate volume of credit or
the amount demanded by individual firms.

Whereas bank deposits (accompanied by documents
certifying a transaction's relation to the plan) are
the primary means of payment in the state sector,
currency is used by individuals and to a lesser extent
agricultural collectives in their dealings among
themselves and with state-owned units. Thus the
economy has two distinct types of "money", with only a

few legal means of transforming one into the other.
Bank deposits in the state sector are closely monitored
and cannot be used freely. They cannot be turned into
cash except through wage payments in accord with the
plan, agricultural purchases, and small miscellaneous
expenditures. On the other hand a true rationed market
for consumer goods does exist, at which individuals are
free to use their holdings of currency as they please,
though expenditures may be limited by the shortage of
commodities. Money deposited in individuals' bank
accounts in principle can be freely withdrawn, except
for time deposits which are supposedly frozen until
their term is up. Savings accounts are the only
financial assets individuals can legally own. Money
belonging to private individuals cannot be used to
purchase important means of production. Moreover, some
consumer goods are formally rationed, in which case
cash plus ration coupons rather than cash alone are
needed to make purchases. Sometimes these same items
may be bought at legal free markets where prices are
allowed to fluctuate and invariably are higher than
official prices. Individuals are not permitted to
write checks.

   In the state sector banks can theoretically
exercise supervision over all microeconomic units,
which automatically translates into macroeconomic
control. In the private sector, however, bank actions
are essentially macroeconomic and nonmandatory in
nature. The main objective is to control inflationary
pressures. This goal is considered accomplished when
the amount of currency outstanding is appropriate given
the (desired) velocity of circulation and the total
value of available consumer goods supplies. Given the
existence of substantial excess demand in the first
place, the hope in actual practice is simply not to
exacerbate inflationary pressures. This can be accomplished by ensuring that the increase in purchasing
power of individuals is "validated" by an appropriate
increase in the quantity of consumer goods for sale.

   The limited number of channels by which currency
enters and leaves circulation are monitored in the
bank's cash plan.[7] Outflow of currency from banks
results mainly from enterprise wage payments (which are
entirely in cash) and state purchases of agricultural
products. Both of these can be strongly influenced by
changes in aggregate or sectoral levels of bank credit.
Individuals' and collectives' purchases of goods and
services from the state sector as well as net increases
in savings deposits are the principal means by which
currency returns to banks. The idea that money in
individuals' bank accounts does not represent demand
for commodities at first sight seems incorrect. But in

China at present over 75 percent of these deposits are
fixed-term time deposits,[8] so it may have some plausi-
bility if one is making a distinction akin to that
between M1 and M2. On the other hand, money in time
deposits probably represents pent-up demand for
consumer durables.

The real fault in the reasoning behind socialist
cash planning is the assumption that private savings
are voluntary, in the sense that individuals do have a
choice between putting money in a bank account or
spending it on goods that are freely available at
existing state-fixed prices. If this is not true, a
balanced cash plan does not necessarily mean that
inflationary pressures are absent, and a large increase
in currency outstanding may not be a sign of
(repressed) inflation if people are simultaneously
drawing down their bank balances.

Banks in theory can control the total amount
of enterprise wage payments because one of their
responsibilities is supervision of disbursements from
the wage fund. Credit to some extent can influence the
total wage bill by affecting an enterprise's scale of
operations. It has an even stronger impact on
purchases of agricultural commodities, since state
commercial units depend mainly on loans for their
working capital. Banks can act directly to increase
the attractiveness of financial savings to the private
sector by raising interest rates, providing better
service, or expanding the banking network. The total
quantity of industrial consumer goods produced and sold
can drastically affect currency flows, but this is
presumably decided at top levels of Party and
government and must be taken as exogenous from the
point of view of cash planning. Bank credit for light
industry conceivably could result in a net decrease in
currency in circulation and thus serve as an effective
anti-inflation measure.

Bank loans to state-owned industry and commerce
are a means of changing the amount of currency in
circulation. At the same time credit is the most
powerful tool and sanction that banks have to direct
the economic activities of enterprises. But in the
classic Stalinian model credit is flawed as a tool for
managing the economy. There are several reasons for
this, each in itself sufficient to seriously weaken
banks' ability to make loan decisions independently.
The conditions under which credit can be granted are
specified strictly and in detail; it is nearly
impossible for a bank to refuse to make a loan to an
enterprise that meets all the relevant conditions.
Credit is granted almost automatically based on
enterprise credit plans and inventories of goods. The

threat to withhold credit is largely empty if it brings
into doubt the continued viability of a firm. Enterprises can respond to a credit crunch by delaying
payments to their creditors, causing an increase in
involuntary trade credit.[9] Bankruptcy solely for lack
of short-term credit is almost never a serious possibility. Perhaps the supervisory organ will guarantee
additional loans to the failing enterprise, as commonly
occurs in the Soviet Union,[10] or political pressure
will be brought to bear by local authorities to force
the bank to grant more credit, which has often been the
case in China.[11] Other bank sanctions like penalty
interest rates, freezing accounts, impounding funds to
pay accumulated debts, and refusal to handle business
are likely to be ineffective for the same reason.
     The banking system in a command economy to a large
extent lacks the tools with which to achieve its main
objectives. Plan fulfillment in the state sector can
be monitored, but enforcement must come from elsewhere.
The bank has a substantial degree of control over only
one of the channels that together determine the amount
of currency in circulation: individuals' savings
accounts. The banks' ability to keep track of the
soundness of enterprise financial management depends on
a number of factors, but even with accurate information
flows there is little they can do to force
improvements.
     In the ideal model of a command economy the bank-
ing system plays no role in financing fixed investment,
which is funded entirely by the state budget. It only
finances a small part of investment in circulating
capital: most of that is provided by the state budget
as well. Private savings are absorbed in order to
combat inflation rather than to increase investment.
Therefore the banking system should not be viewed as a
true financial intermediary.

CHINESE DEPARTURES FROM THE SOVIET MODEL

     Chinese scholarly articles almost invariably
assign a dual role to the banking system. It is
supposed to "encourage" economic development, but at
the same time it should "supervise" the activities of
economic units. The supervisory aspect of bank
responsibilities has often been chronically neglected
in favor of providing wholehearted support for production activities. Banks have been viewed simply as
suppliers of funds, and the distinction between bank
loans and fiscal allocations in many cases was lost on
their recipients. This disdain for financial restrictions which would temper the mass enthusiasm of

lower-level units was prevalent during the Great Leap
Forward and the decade starting with the Cultural
Revolution. It has pervaded Chinese banking policy to
such an extent that the institutional integrity of the
PBC was threatened and its organizational network
partially dismantled in the early and mid-1970s. Over
a much longer period of time the PBC did not have
control over the appointment, transfer, promotion, and
dismissal of its own personnel in branch offices.
Financial discipline was lax, and even the sound
financial accounting practices essential for accurate
monitoring of economic activity by banks or other
organizations were neglected.

The one-sided view of the banking system as
merely supplier of funds to serve production and its
continuing legacy constitute an important Chinese
departure from the basic Soviet model. The Maoist
disdain for bank work was part of a more general attack
on financial indicators (profits) and material
incentives. The effects of this were felt throughout
the economy. Perhaps most important, there was a
marked deterioration in the statistical system, from
which it has not yet entirely recovered, and loss of
information gathering, processing, and recording
ability in enterprises themselves.

The departures discussed above started only with
the Great Leap Forward in 1958. The Chinese financial
system and financial policies as they developed during
the First Five Year Plan (1953-1957) consciously emulated the Soviet Union. As a result institutional
structure and basic modes of thought about finance were
very similar to those in the USSR. Differences did
exist, however, because of the relatively large private
sector remaining in China at the time, the importance
of agriculture, and the underdeveloped condition of the
economy. Before it could become a "monobank" the PBC
had to help control inflation and promote the socialization of firms and collectivization of the countryside. The large proportion of national income
generated in the agricultural sector combined with
relatively insignificant budgetary investment in
it during the 1950s meant that to some extent the
banking system was forced to fill the vaccuum. The
periodic attempts to set up an agricultural bank, the
development of rural credit cooperatives, and the
collectivization of agriculture itself were all
responses to this problem. The underdeveloped nature
of China's economy affected the evolving banking system
in a number of ways. It meant that there were a huge
number of small enterprises using a wide range of
techniques, making it very difficult to include them
under detailed central planning. Profit rates varied

enormously within and across industries, making it infeasible to impose high turnover taxes as the principal means of revenue collection. Skilled, politically reliable personnel were scarce; this meant that staffing needs of government organizations supervising the economy were not met or quality of employees was poor. Since the state banking system grew by nearly 600 percent in terms of number of employees between early 1950 and December 1952 and nearly doubled in the following two years,[12] the latter almost certainly was a problem. Personnel problems also plagued the rural credit cooperatives during their hectic expansion in 1954. An underdeveloped communications network may have further contributed to the difficulties of banks and other organizations in supervising economic activity.

It is interesting to note that many of these features of the Chinese economy are still present today. There is an extremely large number of industrial enterprises, over 380,000 in all,[13] running the gamut in size, technology, and profitability. To a large extent this industrial structure has been fostered by conscious policy. The banking system is plagued by the problem of untrained, low-quality personnel. Agriculture remains a bottleneck; investment in it has been uncoordinated and often has earned low returns. Recently a private sector of sorts has blossomed; more important, various forms of joint ventures and even joint stock, limited liability companies have proliferated. In dealing with these new forms of ownership the banks must use methods different from those appropriate for the state-owned sector.

All in all, the legacy of China's banking system in 1976 was one of fundamental weakness. Internally the PBC was highly centralized in terms of its professional duties. Credit and cash plans were handed down through the hierarchy with little room for the exercise of local initiative. On the other hand crucial personnel decisions as well as political work were under the jurisdiction of the local Party Committees in the areas where bank branches were located. The orientation of employees naturally reflected this and often made local banks little more than "treasuries" for local governments. To a lesser extent this phenomenon also existed at the national level during the period when the PBC was subordinated to the Ministry of Finance. In China the flaws inherent in the Stalinian view of the role of the banking system were magnified by institutional weakness, ideological disdain, and lack of regard for accurate financial accounting.

INFLATION CONTROL

China's banking system accomplished a great
deal during the 1949-1957 period. Control of the
hyperinflation inherited from the previous regime in
1949 was perhaps its greatest achievement. The banking
system also helped dampen inflationary pressures during
the rapid industrialization of the First Five Year
Plan. Successful control of inflation in retail prices
continued until 1979. According to official statistics
the retail price index rose at an average annual rate
of less than 0.8 percent between 1952 and 1978, while
the index of list prices at state commercial units rose
even more slowly.[14] Though different observers dis-
agree on the exact rate of inflation, all agree that it
has been quite low and has not threatened economic
stability. There is also no reason to believe that
there was rapid inflation in unofficial, market-deter-
mined prices over the long term, though significant
fluctuations may have occurred from year to year. A
steady, high rate of inflation in free market prices
would have soon undermined the whole system of state-
fixed prices and rationing, either destroying it or
forcing periodic upward revisions. The fact that
neither of these occurred suggests that though the
official prices are clearly not equilibrium prices,
inflationary pressures in the consumer goods market
have not been increasing rapidly over time. Excess
demand for producer goods has been much more of a
problem, though it did not result in large price
increases until recently. Repressed inflation in this
sector is mainly the result of government investment
policies and the economic system itself rather than the
actions of the banking system. Even large price
increases for producer goods are not likely to dampen
excess demand, which is based on political and administrative behavior as much as on economic criteria.[15]
There are several possible reasons for China's success
in preventing significant inflation. It is beyond the
scope of this study to assess their relative importance, so we will merely list the different explanatory
factors and comment on the mechanisms by which they
worked. Because of the complexities and ambiguities
involved in consideration of inflation in the producer
goods sector, we will concentrate on factors determining retail prices of consumer goods.
Chinese price-setting behavior has striven for
stability in official prices of the most important
basic consumption goods. Cost-based pricing has not
been mechanically applied.[16] Instead, upward
fluctuations in costs have been counterbalanced by
downward shifts in profits, tax rates, and in some

cases even interest rates on loans to producers or commercial units.[17] Though this behavior is the proximate cause of price stability, it cannot succeed unless costs are prevented from continuously rising. Otherwise profits would turn into deficits and increasing subsidies would be required, which apparently did not occur to a marked extent before the late 1970s.

In the Soviet Union wage inflation was a major force behind the serious price inflation that occurred during the period of rapid industrialization. Except for occasional wage readjustments and, more recently, general wage hikes, average wages in China's urban areas have remained remarkably stable. As can be seen from Table 8, average nominal wages in the state sector declined by 5.5 percent between 1957 and 1977. Rural incomes until recently have fluctuated with the harvest and therefore have not been a source of inflationary pressure. Several factors have contributed to long-term wage stability in China. Labor is allocated administratively; workers are not free to move from job to job seeking higher wages. Thus competition for workers has played almost no role in determining wages. Conscious policy has held down urban wages to avoid enlarging urban-rural differentials in living standards. For long periods bonus payments to individual workers were prohibited, preventing increases in wage costs from this source. On the demand side stable prices combined with increasing participation rates allowed the average urban family to increase its real standard of living somewhat, despite the stagnation in earnings per worker. Though the average price paid by the government for agricultural products rose somewhat during the period under consideration, agricultural production costs apparently rose faster, meaning that inflationary pressures from this source were dampened somewhat. Changes in the prices of other raw material inputs for the production of consumer goods appear not to have had a significant net inflationary effect on costs.

China has striven to maintain a budget surplus in most years. This combined with an innovation developed during the 1950s has been a powerful force in dampening inflationary pressures. The state budget since the mid-1950s has included an appropriation for "bank credit funds," in recent breakdowns lumped together with allocations of working capital for enterprises.[18] Since bank loans are limited only by the plan (or by increases in inventories if the credit plan is exceeded), granting budgetary funds for this purpose seems inappropriate. What it does, though, is ensure that a portion of revenues are not spent directly, and that possible increases in credit are offset to some extent by decreases in budgetary expenditures compared to what they otherwise would have been. This method works well when budget surpluses are maintained. If there is a budget deficit, however, the first inclination of authorities in trying to regain balance is to cut expenditures for bank credit funds and working capital of enterprises. Since changes in the former may not affect the level of bank credit at all and cuts in the latter most likely will be offset by increases in bank loans for working capital, budget balance achieved in this way could be illusory: the inflationary impact may not be diminished.

Efforts by the banking system itself to control inflation have focussed on the quantity of currency in circulation. During the 1950s high interest rates and even prizes were used to attract more savings deposits from the population. The PBC, however, could not effectively control the aggregate amount of credit it granted, meaning that it essentially had to influence currency outstanding by increasing withdrawals from circulation rather than limiting currency leaving banks.[19] Loans to support state agricultural purchases have also been cited as a deflationary measure that the banks can use. In the 1950s these loans, which allowed commercial departments to purchase agricultural products and were repaid with the proceeds of sales of such products to urban consumers, probably had a deflationary impact because of their rapid turnover and the high price mark-ups involved. As a result the whole process resulted in net withdrawal of currency from circulation.[20] These mark-ups have since disappeared, and commerce in agricultural commodities must now be subsidized by the state. Therefore the impact of credit for agricultural purchases is inflationary - more currency is released into circulation in rural areas than is absorbed from urban areas. If for some reason inflationary pressures are worse in urban areas than in rural areas, the policy might still make sense from the viewpoint of inflation control, but this is not likely to be true. In any case, provision of adequate supplies of farm products to the urban population is a higher priority for the government than limiting currency in circulation.

China's success in inflation control is also attributed to insulation from the fluctuations of the world market.[21] Chinese authors assert that "planned and proportionate development of the national economy" is a major reason why the country has not suffered from inflation. In view of the massive sectoral and structural imbalances that have accompanied China's economic development, this argument is unacceptable. One author, in comparing China with other developing

economies, states that the country was able to control
inflation because the government placed top priority on
supplying adequate amounts of basic necessities to the
entire population, and devised institutions capable of
ensuring that this would happen.[22] This explanation
does not go deep enough in searching for underlying
causes, but points in the right general direction.
Government policies and institutions have been as
important in preventing significant inflation in China
as "monetary" factors like the amount of currency in
circulation or even balanced budgets.

Three salient points emerge from this discussion:
(1) China was remarkably successful in controlling
inflation from 1949 to 1976; (2) the banking system had
relatively little to do with this except in the early
1950s; and (3) some of the tools used to fight inflation in the past have lost their effectiveness in the
present situation.

POLITICAL AND SPECIFIC SECTORAL OBJECTIVES

China's banking system probably had its greatest
success in guiding the Chinese economy when the private
sector was still a significant part of urban industry
and commerce in the early 1950s. It played an active
role in helping eliminate the hyperinflation inherited
from the previous regime. After the private banking
sector itself was nationalized or brought under PBC
control, the latter promoted the socialization of
industry and commerce by means of various measures.
These included discrimination against the private
sector and positive inducements for firms to become
joint state-private enterprises. The collectivization
of agriculture was heavily supported by loans. But
once banks came to deal primarily with socialized
economic units, restrictions they attempted to impose
became politically unpopular. Unlike private firms,
state enterprises could make their complaints heard by
Party and government cadres in a position to influence
bank decisions. Though the effective subordination of
local bank branches to local Party Committees did not
occur until 1958, problems in implementing bank
supervision were already common during the First Five
Year Plan period.

After the 1950s the banking system was called
upon to promote development of specific sectors of the
economy, by means of special loans and/or favorable
interest rates. Agriculture was the most favored
sector, as can be seen from the present structure of
interest rates (Table 9). In particular, loans for
agricultural equipment purchases and grain enterprises

carry the lowest interest rates of any bank loans to
nonbank entities. Various types of loans subsidized by
local governments have been interest-free, making them
little different from fiscal appropriations. Indeed,
the same can be said about agricultural loans as a
whole:

> As for agricultural loans, they have actually
> been rendered as financial appropriations in
> a disguised form. It is not only that people just
> raise agricultural loans and do not pay them back,
> but that some people even go as far as to advocate
> that all outstanding debts be remitted.[23]

Repayment problems have plagued agricultural
loans, both short-term and long-term. According to one
report, at the end of 1979 the total value of agricultural loans which could not or would not be repaid when
due exceeded Y 10 billion.[24] This was over half the
total value of all loans to rural areas by banks and
credit cooperatives outstanding at that time (Tables 1
and 3). If agricultural loans subsidized by the
localities are added to the total figure the proportion
might drop somewhat; even so, it is alarmingly high,
and the efficiency with which loans were utilized must
have been low. Current policy hopes to speed turnover
and improve returns by restricting issuance of new
agricultural loans.[25]

An experimental program involving small technical
innovation loans to Shanghai's light and textile
industries was a precursor of the recent expansion of
the scope of credit in the Chinese economy.[26] Run by
the Shanghai branch of the People's Construction Bank
of China (PCBC), it was started in 1964 and interrupted
between 1970 and 1972. After that it continued and
expanded. Until June 1979 loans were interest-free;
after that the bank charged 0.3 percent per month for
loans of less than one year duration, 0.42 percent for
those to be repaid in more than one year. The average
turnover of funds between 1972 and 1979 was thirteen
months, and the average value of each loan was
Y 34,000. By the end of 1979 the total balance of
loans outstanding was Y 110 million. Returns on
investments made with these loans were generally high;
from 1972 to 1978 only 1.15 percent of the loan
projects, accounting for 1.18 percent of total funds
loaned, failed to make repayment from the proceeds of
the projects undertaken. The semi-fiscal character of
the program is illustrated by the fact that these
unsuccessful loans were repaid by state appropriations.
The experiment clearly was successful, though this
probably was due more to the economic environment of

Shanghai than the quality or design of the program
itself.

A similar program was instituted on a nationwide
basis in 1975. By 1977 certain problems had cropped
up.[27] Localities were arbitrarily increasing their
small technical innovation loans far beyond centrally
determined targets. Recipients of loans were diverting
them to use in large capital construction projects.
Repayments were commonly made from funds other than the
increased income resulting from the projects. These
difficulties are similar to those that affect various
loan programs today.

The PCBC also granted special loans to support
improvements in quality, variety, and packaging of
industrial goods produced for export. This program was
started in the mid-1960s; after an interruption
presumably caused by the Cultural Revolution, it was
revived and expanded in the 1970s. In contrast to the
small loan program for technical innovations, these
carried an interest rate of 0.42 percent per month,
with repayments of interest required every quarter.[28]
Results were poor, even in Shanghai. There about
one-third of the loans were not repaid on time: as of
the first half of 1978 almost 5,000 projects tying up a
total investment of over Y 1 billion were under
construction. There were widespread shortages of raw
materials, equipment, and construction force.[29] This
is not surprising in view of the fact that no raw
materials or equipment for these projects were
allocated by the state plan; local governments were
supposed to make arrangements for these on their
own.[30]

These bank operations to promote specific goals
were generally small, with the important exception of
loans for agricultural mechanization. They were in
most cases handled by the PCBC and used fiscal
appropriations as their source of funds. They seem
especially insignificant when compared with the
proliferation of special loan programs and reduced
interest rates for specific categories of loans since
1978, handled for the most part by the PBC or
specialized banks under its aegis.

The most important of the new programs is
the PBC's short- and medium-term loans to finance the
purchase of equipment by industrial enterprises. By
the end of 1981 the total value of such loans
outstanding reached Y 8.375 billion (Table 1). At
the end of the third quarter of 1982 the figure was
Y 12.135 billion,[31] and by the end of the year it
had reached Y 15.198 billion. The returns on some of
the projects financed by these loans have reportedly
been high. According to one source, Y 3.56 billion in

such loans extended in 1980 generated an additional
gross output value of Y 4.5 billion in 1980 alone.[32]
Various sources provide foreign exchange loans
to support production for export, including a program
by the BOC and loans using foreign exchange retained by
the localities. Foreign exchange loans are often
paired with loans in Chinese currency, which cover
domestic financing needs (so-called two loans'
programs.)[33] Urban collective enterprises formed by
unemployed youth could borrow from banks at 0.36
percent during their first two years of business,
compared with the regular rate for collectives before
1982 of 0.42 percent (Table 9). Grain enterprises had
interest rates on their circulating capital loans
slashed from 0.42 percent to 0.21 percent in 1978,[34]
though this was more to improve their financial situation than to promote expansion of their activities.
Loans for production by individual commune members in
the countryside and more recently to urban individual
businesses have been encouraged.[35] No explicit
interest subsidy has been granted by banks, but in some
rural areas the local government pays interest
costs.[36] Most recently, the PBC has lowered interest
rates on both circulating capital and fixed investment
loans to enterprises that specialize in minority
nationalities' handicraft production and trade.[37]
Thus in the past several years numerous special
loan programs and interest subsidies have been used to
further the authorities' new sectoral goals. Though
there is some continuity with innovations in the 1960s
and early 1970s, the scale of the new programs is much
larger. Private financial returns on many projects
supported by these loans, particularly small ones,
appear to be very high.

EFFICIENCY IN ALLOCATION AND USE
OF WORKING CAPITAL LOANS

Except in agriculture, nearly all bank loans prior
to 1979 were used to finance working capital requirements of enterprises. Even in 1980, circulating
capital loans by the PBC and specialized banks managed
by it comprised at the very least 78 percent of the
total value of net new credit extended. They accounted
for at least 91 percent of the total value of loans
outstanding at the end of that year.[38] In evaluating
the past economic performance of the banking system,
then, we must focus on working capital funds and their
physical counterpart, inventories and goods in process,
rather than the financing of fixed investment, over
which banks had little control. In assessing the

efficiency of investment in working capital a number of
aspects are relevant: (1) the total size of inventories in relation to economic activity; (2) the
proportion of measured economic growth that is due only
to inventory accumulation; (3) the rate of turnover of
inventories, and the percentage of goods that remain
stockpiled for long periods of time: (4) imbalances in
inventory holdings, particularly the relative proportions in the hands of producers, users, and trading
organizations; and (5) the percentage of inventories
that consist of substandard or unmarketable goods. For
many of these indicators the financial side must also
be considered, generally by substituting the words
"circulating capital funds" for physical inventories.
Available data indicate that performance and results
have been rather poor. Inefficiency in the allocation
and use of working capital is a typical problem in
centrally planned economies. To a large extent the PBC
was unable rather than unwilling to control the growth
of circulating capital loans and inventories. For this
reason what follows should be viewed as a critique of
many parts of the economic system rather than the
banking system taken alone.

One of the most important principles of socialist
bank credit is that loans must be secured by physical
resources in the possession of the borrower. This
inventory criterion turns out in practice to mean that
the level of inventories to a large extent determines
the level of credit and not vice versa. At least at
the margin, inventories can create credit, which is
almost automatically granted when goods are purchased.
It should not be surprising if inventories rise rapidly
under such a system, since they are essentially cost-
less to hold. This tendency is strongly reinforced by
problems with shortages of material inputs, which cause
enterprises and supervisory departments at all levels
to hold large stocks against future needs. The inventory criterion for bank credit allows this type of
behavior to go unchecked.

While producers stockpile material inputs against
future needs, on the output side commercial units may
end up holding large inventories of goods that cannot
be sold. Unless banks exercise close supervision it is
nearly impossible for them to ascertain whether goods
purchased from industrial producers by the commercial
system are marketable and of good quality. Thus they
do grant loans to purchase goods that cannot be sold.
Stockpiles of unmarketable goods will eventually be
manifested in a unit's inability to repay the loan
which they secured, but it is much more difficult to
recall these loans than it was to grant them in the
first place. Thus both excessive growth of inventories

and large holdings of unmarketable or substandard goods
are encouraged by the way in which credit is granted.
Failure to give loans for purchases of these products,
however, sets off a chain reaction whereby the producer
builds up a large stock of its own unsold products, for
which it may request credit; if that is refused its
solvency and continued operations are threatened, in
which case the enterprise's managing department would
step in.

In China working capital funds have grown
considerably faster than output. The average value of
circulating capital funds per Y 100 of output value
by state-owned industrial enterprises rose from
Y 19.4 in 1957 to Y 25.5 in 1965 and Y 33.4 in 1975,
followed by a decline to Y 32.0 in 1978 and Y 30.1 in
1980.[39] Even the economically advanced city of
Shanghai showed a similar though less marked deterioration, from Y 15.63 per Y 100 of output value by
state-owned industrial enterprises to Y 21.37 in
1976.[40] These increases are far greater than what
reasonably could be attributed to changes in the
sectoral composition of industrial output during the
period. Much of the rise in the circulating capital-
total output value ratio was caused by bank loans
rather than budgetary grants of working capital. In
1953 bank credit made up only 16.7 percent of the total
circulating funds of industrial enterprises; by 1979
the figure had risen to 34.6 percent. Among commercial
enterprises the amount of circulating funds per Y 100
of sales rose from Y 38 in 1957 to Y 44 in 1979.[41]
About 82 percent of commercial circulating funds in
1979 were in the form of bank loans, so again credit
must have been the major cause of the rise in the
working capital-sales ratio. It is more difficult to
assess historical trends in the case of material supply
enterprises and foreign trade units, but we do know
that in 1979 67 percent of the circulating funds of the
former and 87 percent of those of the latter consisted
of bank loans.[42]

Inventories of specific categories of goods have
become very large, though here it is hard to distin-
guish between pre- and post-1976 trends. China's
stockpile of rolled steel rose from 12 million tons at
the end of 1976 to over 19.5 million tons at the end of
1980, before dropping to around 18 million tons in late
1982.[43] These figures compare with total rolled
steel output of 27.2 million tons in 1980 and 26.7 million tons in 1981.[44] Total inventories of machinery
and electrical equipment at the end of June 1980 were
valued at Y 61.9 billion, amounting to well over one
year's production.[45] According to one account, 5-10
percent of these products will have to be written off

and about 40 percent will have to be disposed of at
reduced prices.[46] Even in late 1982 stockpiles of
machinery and electrical equipment totalled Y 58 billion.[47] Stockpiles of unsold goods for export in
1980 were worth over Y 10 billion, more than 36 percent
of the value of commodities actually exported in that
year.[48] At the end of June 1978 the total value of
agricultural machinery held in stock by sales companies
was Y 5.8 billion, including poor quality and even
useless items originally priced at over Y 1.58 billion
- 17.2 percent of the total inventory.[49]

There is also evidence of severe imbalances
between stocks held by producers and those in the
possession of commercial units. In late 1978 or early
1979, 60.18 percent of China's total inventory of
rolled steel was held by production and construction
enterprises and another 21.39 percent by the supply
departments of those production and construction units.
Another 1.96 percent was in steel plants, and only
16.47 percent of the total national inventory was in
the hands of material supply departments charged with
purchasing and selling rolled steel. Similarly only
9.48 percent of the total stockpile of machinery and
electrical equipment was held by material supply
departments and 5.58 percent by producers; the rest
belonged to users.[50] Concentration of inventories of
capital goods and intermediate products in the hands of
purchasers rather than sellers is the typical pattern
in centrally planned economies, and China has been no
exception.

We do not have reliable information on the proportion of China's economic growth that results from
inventory accumulation or from production of substandard products. In 1978, however, many localities
stopped reporting substandard products as part of total
industrial output value. This change reportedly
caused the 1978 growth rate of China's total industrial
output value (13.5 percent) to drop significantly
compared with the 1977 figure of 14.1 percent.[51]
Somewhere between 0.5 percent and 1 percent of China's
total industrial output value in 1978 may therefore
have consisted of substandard products. These most
likely included only those rejected by commercial
departments and not poor quality items that were
purchased by them anyway.

The proportion of overdue loans is another
indication of problems with excessive stockpiling by
producers or the holding of unmarketable inventories
by commercial units for long periods of time. In early
1980 about 70 percent of all loans to industrial
enterprises in the Inner Mongolian Autonomous Region
were overdue.[52] This is an extreme example, but

numerous other reports indicate that overdue loans
comprised a significant proportion of total bank credit
in various localities.

All in all, the fragmentary evidence presented
here strongly suggests that bank loans to finance
working capital did not promote economic efficiency.
The way in which credit was extended encouraged
excessive inventory accumulation as well as production
and storage of defective goods. This caused a great
amount of waste and to some extent inflated figures on
China's economic performance. New policies pursued
since 1976 may have begun to have modest results, but
the problems discussed in this section remain serious.
It remains to be seen whether strict administrative
controls and economic sanctions (e.g. penalty interest
rates for overdue loans or those financing excessive
stockpiles) will change the picture.

4
Banking Reforms, 1976–1982: Background and Chronological Review

BACKGROUND

Changes in China's financial system that have occurred since the almost simultaneous death of Mao and fall of the "Gang of Four" in 1976 must be seen in the context of overall economic reform and the leadership's new priorities for economic development. This section will briefly discuss Chinese economic reforms in general, while those that follow will outline the main financial reforms and review the progress of their implementation. Chapter 5 will analyse and evaluate the most important financial reforms in more detail.

There are at least four main directions in Chinese national economic policy during the 1976–1982 period: (1) Soviet-style rapid growth oriented primarily toward heavy industry and steel; (2) readjustment; (3) economic reform per se; and (4) administrative decentralization. Recent policy changes are not entirely new in content, but taken together and given the fact that serious attempts at implementation are being made, they constitute a substantial departure from anything that had been seen previously in the PRC. Behind the changes in concrete economic policies lie even more important reversals in attitudes about the goals of economic activity and the proper indicators of economic development.

At the beginning of the period under consideration, the predominant view was that economic development is measured by growth in output of strategic commodities like steel. Now it is generally recognized that per capita consumption and living standards are much better indicators. The shift from production to consumption as the goal of economic activity has had an important effect on economic policies. At a deeper level, objective economic laws have come to be seen as

having universal significance; they cannot be violated
without paying a heavy price, even by superhuman
efforts called forth by Maoist genius and mass political campigns. The focus of activity has shifted from
political struggle to economic modernization.

Turning now to concrete policies, the first main
direction was dominant immediately after the ouster of
the Gang of Four and was thoroughly discredited by late
1979. In simple terms it saw rapid growth of key
commodities like steel and grain, financed by a high
rate of investment, as the means to economic development. In recognition of China's lagging and to a large
extent stagnant technology, one new ingredient was
added: massive imports of the most modern plants and
equipment from the West would raise Chinese industry's
technological level to advanced world standards. It
was envisioned that these imports would be paid for
largely with rapidly expanding oil exports, though in
the short term a considerable amount of foreign debt
could be incurred. Of course raising the technological
level and improving the efficiency of existing enterprises was not entirely neglected. But the methods
used to accomplish this purpose at first were mainly
directives and mass campaigns. These policies were
fully expressed in the ambitious Ten Year Plan.[1] Some
of its targets would have been nearly impossible to
achieve, others were only moderately ambitious, but as
a whole it embodied the principle of taut planning.
Investment was to be concentrated in large projects
primarily in the heavy industrial sector. This strand
of economic policy closely resembles the traditional
Soviet model, which was emulated in China during the
First Five-Year Plan period. In its goals it constituted a more realistic version of the Great Leap
Forward, but with imports of advanced technology
substituted for mass enthusiasm and local initiative.

As the unified "state book-keeping organ,"[2] the
banking system had a significant role to play in this
scenario. It needed a certain degree of independence
in order to monitor plan fulfillment and financial
management throughout the economy. Thus the emphasis
in this period was on institutional rebuilding of the
banking system without internal reform, and on restoring enterprise financial accounting practices to the
point where accurate information was available for
supervisory organs. Economic criteria and administrative regulations were to govern bank decisions on
credit and other important matters, as opposed to
orders emanating from local government and Party cadres
outside the banking system. Bank auditing of enterprises was restored; attempts were made to instill
better accounting procedures and detect and punish

deliberate misuse of accounting categories or fraud.
The status of accountants was raised, their independence guaranteed. Profits once again became an
accepted indicator of enterprise performance, though
not yet a source of material benefits for firms or
their personnel.
    Many of these measures strengthening the banking
system and financial accounting in general do not
conflict with other strands of economic policy that
came into vogue later. Thus they by and large survived
the demise of the Ten Year Plan and the priorities it
represented. Fortunately for China, the phase of
overly ambitious planning did not last long enough to
give the country an unmanageable foreign debt problem.
By late 1978 or early 1979 it became apparent that the
goals of the Ten Year Plan could not be achieved and
that after an initial spurt economic growth was
beginning to slow down as numerous bottlenecks asserted
themselves. Growing foreign debts were distasteful to
many Chinese policymakers, particularly since oil
exports to pay for the imported technology did not
materialize in the required quantities. All these
considerations as well as internal political realign-
ments eventually doomed the "big push with foreign
technology" scenario.
    The second set of policies essentially replaced
the first; it has dominated macro-level national
economic policymaking in rhetoric since June 1979, and
increasingly in implementation as well. It advocates a
balanced growth strategy and in the present situation
readjustment to rectify imbalances built up over the
years by mistaken policies. These imbalances include
(in rough order of importance): excessive accumulation
at the expense of consumption; excessive emphasis on
(and investment in) industry at the expense of agriculture; within industry neglect of light industry; over-
emphasis on productive investment at the expense of
nonproductive investment (housing, schools, public
facilities, etc.); and within the category of productive investment lack of attention to investment in
energy and infrastructure. The notion of and
justification behind taut planning is completely
rejected. Plans must be realisitic in terms of the
material and financial resources of the country; they
should include some slack for contingencies. In the
financial sphere readjustment implies balancing the
state budget by means of expenditure cuts, especially
in appropriations for capital construction. Tighter
controls over credit and currency issuance also should
be imposed.
    Readjustment has primarily macroeconomic concerns,
and its dictates have been enforced mainly by administrative measures. This is especially true of the

"stick" side - orders to shut down plants, force them to change their line of products, or merge with other enterprises. Capital construction projects also have been cancelled or postponed by direct orders passed through the government administrative hierarchy. On the "carrot" side, encouraging the expansion of neglected sectors, economic incentives play a more important role. Examples are the PBC's massive loan program for small investment projects by the light and textile industries, higher state purchase prices for agricultural products, devaluation of the domestic currency for internal accounting purposes, making production for export more profitable, and low interest loans to collective enterprises formed by jobless educated youth. Nevertheless, the overall focus is on changing macro-proportions in the economy rather than on the individual micro-level units and their decisions.

The implications of readjustment for the banking system are mixed. On the one hand, banks can be the instruments used to promote the expansion of neglected sectors through ad-hoc measures. On the other hand, use of economic criteria by banks in making decisions must not take precedence over the dictates of readjustment. The banks' independence must not be allowed to interfere with macro-level priorities. Still, accurate financial accounting and monitoring by banks are necessary to determine which enterprises in a sector to shut down. Moreover, banks must be strong enough to resist both enterprises and their higher-level supporters who may try to avoid cutbacks by obtaining financing through bank loans. They must also be able to refuse to finance projects for which resources are lacking or required complementary invest-ments are not being made.

The third main policy direction also represents a reaction to the failure of the ambitious growth strategy of 1977-1978. A great many new policies are being tried out or widely implemented under the general rubric of economic reform. Several unifying themes tie together what might otherwise seem a diverse set of measures applied in piecemeal and sometimes inconsis-tent ways in different sectors. The focus is invari-ably the microeconomy, the basic economic units and the environments in which they operate. Enterprises in industry and basic accounting units in agriculture, even individuals in certain spheres of activity, are to be given the authority to make meaningful decisions and must be responsible for the consequences of their actions. They should be guided in their activities by material incentives as well as by orders and detailed plans. Profits earned and retained by economic units

become more than just an accounting category and
success indicator; they are transformed into the
material reward an enterprise receives for good
performance. For profits to be meaningful firms should
be free to sell at least some portion of their output
independently from the deliveries called for in the
plan. This requires markets or some other means of
bringing buyers and sellers together on a voluntary
basis. For profits accurately to reflect enterprise
performance prices must have some meaningful relation
to scarcity values in the economy. Hence the need for
price reform. In particular, enterprises should "pay"
for all of their inputs, including capital.

Different forms of ownership are now tolerated,
even given encouragement and material support if they
can perform more efficiently than state-owned units in
a given sphere of activity. Collective and individual
economic units have proliferated as a result. The past
few years have also seen the emergence of integrated
operations and joint stock companies of various kinds,
some of which permit purchases of shares by individuals.[3] As a result what very loosely could be
described as an unorganized capital market of sorts has
arisen, in the sense that demanders and suppliers of
capital can now get together and make trades on a
voluntary basis. Most of the efficiencies normally
associated with markets are not being realized since
transferability of assets is extremely limited.
Moreover, in China's only partially monetized economy
access to raw materials, physical plant, and land may
determine the value of investments more than monetary
contributions.

The banking system's role in economic reforms is
two-fold and contradictory. It should be supportive,
relaxing restrictive policies that might hinder enterprises from exercising their legitimate decisionmaking
powers. On the other hand banks are supposed to
influence macro-level economic activity indirectly by
means of "economic levers" like interest rates. The
demarcation between restrictions that hinder the expansion of enterprise autonomy and legitimate use of
indirect controls to guide the economy is a fuzzy one.
Furthermore, internal banking reforms that give local
branches more independence and encourage them to become
profit oriented may result in less rather than more
latitude for enterprises in their dealings with the
banking system.

The fourth main policy direction in national
economic policy since 1976 is administrative decentralization, nothing new in essence but in some
respects now being pushed farther than ever before.
Some of the changes involve not only granting more

authority to lower levels in the administrative
hierarchy, but also providing them with certain kinds
of "material incentives" to improve performance.

Fiscal decentralization measures promulgated in
early 1980 gave provincial-level authorities control
over revenues collected locally sufficient to cover
normal expenditures, including capital construction.[4]
Provinces also share in any increase in revenues or the
benefits from economizing on expenditures. The
revenue-sharing proportions, based on 1979 realized
revenue and expenditure figures, in principle will
remain fixed for a period of five years, reducing the
possibility of a "ratchet effect" in the short run. On
the other hand, the effects of shortfalls in revenues
or excessive expenditures will also be borne in part by
the provinces. Provincial budgets are thus no longer
tied completely to the national budget; provinces have
their own sources of funds with some freedom to expand
them in the future.

There is a certain asymmetry in the fact that
provinces whose local revenues exceed their normal
local expenditures get a fixed subsidy, while provinces
with surpluses share specified revenues proportion-
ately. Given certain reasonable assumptions on the way
revenues enter the utility functions of provincial
authorities, the surplus provinces will not maximize
those revenues that they share with the central
government in fixed proportions. On the other hand
provinces receiving fixed subsidies from the center
clearly have an incentive to maximize their local
revenues. A potentially more serious problem stems
from the fact that provinces are responsible for
collecting revenues of the central government which
they don't share in at all. There must be a strong
incentive for them covertly to shift revenues from
these categories into those which they are allowed to
retain in full or in part. This would only exacerbate
the deficit problems of the central government. It
should be noted that for a few provinces the revenue-
sharing system is somewhat different. Guangdong and
Fujian transfer fixed sums to the center each year,
while Beijing, Shanghai, Tianjin, and Jiangsu share
total revenues with the national government.

The 1980 decentralization measures resemble those
of 1958, but go an important step further by including
capital construction as part of normal local expenditures.[5] Moreover, the earlier devolution was to a
large extent rescinded in 1959. References to another
decentralization that occurred in 1970 have appeared in
the Chinese media.

Though there is no sign that the budgetary devolution of 1980 has been entirely retracted, measures

taken in early 1981 to tighten up on readjustment may
have limited its impact. Essentially the central
government has taken back by means of involuntary loans
and Treasury bond sales some of what it originally gave
the provinces as a consequence of fiscal decentralization. This is a common pattern in Chinese economic
reforms of the past several years: the government
first acts to give micro-level units more decisionmaking power and financial autonomy, then uses ad-hoc
administrative measures to counteract the macro-level
consequences.

Significant territorial decentralization occurred
in China's foreign trade management in 1979. Certain
provinces and municipalities are allowed to keep for
their own use varying percentages of the foreign
exchange earned by their exports.[6] In some cases
enterprises are also allowed to retain part of their
foreign exchange earnings directly, while other firms
have it parcelled out to them from the retained
holdings of territorial units. These measures make
unified central control over China's aggregate foreign
exchange transactions more difficult.

As government administrative organizations China's
banks have also undergone significant decentralization.
Local bank branches are now allowed to reallocate loans
among certain categories as long as the sum total still
fits the plan target. More important, if a local
bank's deposits surpass its plan or it economizes on
loans (by speeding turnover, for example), the surplus
can be used to make more loans. The decentralization
of China's banking system will be discussed more fully
in Chapter 5, but it can be pointed out here that it
has much in common with the recent budgetary
devolution.

Though internal decentralization of the banking
system appears to be a popular policy, there is more
controversy over the role bank branches should play in
serving local as opposed to national interests.
Greater decisionmaking power for local banks in some
ways only worsens the dilemma faced by an organization
that is supposed to promote production at the same time
that it supervises the activities of enterprises and
watches out for the interests of the state. One
solution suggested is creation of an industrial and
commercial credit bank separate from the PBC.[7]
Another article advocates establishment of independent
local banks to serve the needs of their communities,
while the PBC retains control over important central
banking functions.[8]

This brief account may make Chinese economic
policies in the past half decade seem more rational and
coordinated than they really were. Some reforms were

poorly planned, and in many cases implementation was
hurried and occurred with inadequate preparation.
Possible consequences were generally not thought out in
advance. As a result ad-hoc measures sometimes
followed one after another with little in the way of
overall coordination. Different actions by the
government have had differing, sometimes conflicting
effects on the banking system. Nevertheless, the
strengthening of China's banks has been a common theme
that runs through most policy prescriptions.

MAIN DIRECTIONS OF BANKING REFORM

There are five main currents in the reform of
China's banking system. One is reassertion of its
independence and organizational integrity, combined
with the establishment or restoration of certain
specialized financial institutions. Attention is
focussed on redefining the relationship between banks
and other supervisory organs responsible for overseeing
the economy.

The second main trend involves strengthening and
transforming the banks' position vis-a-vis their
clients (mainly industrial and commercial enterprises
in the case of the PBC). Bank decisions affecting
clients should be based on independent use of economic
criteria rather than administrative fiat or blind
adherence to detailed plans. "Economic levers" such as
interest rates and repayment terms should partially
supplant directives in guiding the actions of enterprises. Loan agreements should be formalized in economic contracts between bank branches and enterprises.
At the same time the right of banks to make independent
judgments on loan applications and if necessary refuse
to grant credit is strongly affirmed.

The third current, very important from the banking
system's own point of view, is internal decentralization. This has two aspects. Administratively local
bank branches are being given more flexibility in the
important area of credit planning. They are now
allowed to reallocate loans among different categories
of the credit plan, and as mentioned before can use the
proceeds of an increase in deposits or greater efficiency in making planned loans to extend more loans in
their localities. Now considered to be economic units
as well as administrative bodies, bank branches have
been made into independent accounting units, whose
employees are eligible to receive bonuses. Interest is
charged on interbranch deposits and loans, albeit at a
relatively low rate.

Improving the quality of the banking system's
human capital is another major objective. This ties in
closely with a more economic orientation and bonuses
for employees; it also is closely related to the
reassertion of bank independence with regard to
personnel decisions. Better training of new bank
cadres and extensive courses for veteran and leading
personnel are the main means of achieving this goal.
The following report gives both an indication of the
magnitude of this task and its importance to the
banking system:

> A short-term plan and a long-term program
> have been worked out by the People's Bank
> of China to raise the educational level of
> its staff. The short-term plan stipulates
> that before the end of 1983, all leading
> cadres and staff, including new recruits will
> get two-to-six months training on a rotation
> system. In 1980, 68,464 people took the
> two-month vocational training; this is about
> 30 percent of all cadres and workers sche-
> duled for such training. According to the
> long-term program, by 1990 a comprehensive
> college and middle-school education system
> will be set up within the bank so that
> workers' education will be institutional-
> ized. A bank official said that China would
> set up a national education committee within
> the banking system. A college was planned
> for the advanced training of cadres.[9]

The fifth current, closely related to internal
decentralization, involves the most drastic departure
from prereform practice. Bank branches as well as
trust and investment corporations they may set up are
supposed to act as financial intermediaries, bringing
together the idle, surplus funds of economic units and
government organizations and using them to make
investments that will foster local economic development. The key innovation is not the mobilizing of
surplus funds, which is a legitimate though in the
classic Soviet model a relatively unimportant role of
banks. What is really new is the active search for
local investment opportunities and the ability to make
investments in projects that may not be part of the
state plan. For this very reason the future of the
financial intermediary role is still in doubt,
particularly since central authorities are trying to
regain control over investment activities.

CHRONOLOGICAL REVIEW

From 1976 until late 1978 or early 1979, restoring
the independence of the PBC at all levels and strengthening bank supervision of the financial transactions of
enterprises were the main policy focus. The PBC
regained its independent, ministry-level status soon
after the fall of the "Gang of Four." Restoration work
at the lower levels continued for several years. In
1978 a campaign to rectify enterprise financial appropriations, funds, and bank accounts got fully underway.[10] There were also related efforts to get rid of
excessive inventories stockpiled by enterprises, with
only peripheral involvement by banks.[11] The position
and independence of accounting personnel were strengthened by State Council regulations on their functions
and powers, promulgated in the fall of 1978.[12]
Reports of sanctions against deficit enterprises,
ranging from paycuts for staff to temporary shutdowns,
start to appear in 1978.[13] There are hardly any
references to bank involvement in this process, however. In the countryside the main emphasis was on
straightening out the accounts of collectives,
especially encouraging cadres, higher-level units, and
peasants to repay debts and longstanding overdrafts to
production teams.

1979 was the year of reform for the banking system
as well as for the rest of the economy. The initial
impetus and official sanction for thoroughgoing banking reforms was a nationwide meeting of bank branch
directors held by the PBC in Beijing from February 5 to
February 28, 1979. Its minutes were considered so
important that subsequently they were officially
approved by the State Council itself.[14] The recommendations made at the conference were wide ranging and
have been the starting point for discussions of reforms
since then. Therefore it is worthwhile to restate them
in condensed form here. One source which provides a
convenient summary gives them the title "The Four
Transformations and Eight Reforms."[15] The "Four
Transformations" are:

(1) From customarily using purely administrative
     methods in work to using economic means to
     manage the economy and the banks.
(2) From paying insufficient attention to organ-
     izing capital to concentrating on expanding the
     sources of funds and utilizing them well.
(3) From making loans solely on the basis of pro-
     duction plans and commodity circulation plans
     to gradually basing loans on economic con-
     tracts, given implementation of state plans.

(4) From a situation in which banks throughout the country "eat from the same big pot" to implementing enterprise-type management by banks at all levels with strict economic accounting.

The "Eight Reforms" are:

(1) There should be an appropriate rise in interest rates on savings deposits and an increase in the variety of accounts available.

(2) In making loans the policy should be "differential treatment, selection and fostering of the best" (enterprises), based on their implementation of the state plan, fulfillment of their economic contracts, and level of management competence and creditworthiness.

(3) Restoration of various specialized banks and corporations. The Agricultural Bank of China should be restored, and both it and the Bank of China should be placed directly under the State Council, managed on behalf of the latter by the People's Bank. Also advocated are establishment of a national-level printing corporation and restoration of the domestic insurance business of the People's Insurance Company of China.

(4) To fill in the gaps left by state plans, banks should be allowed to make short- and mediumterm loans for equipment purchases. They should be used for construction of small hydroelectric and thermoelectric facilities and for individual items of equipment for existing enterprises.

(5) Change the existing system of credit planning (unified central control over all loans and deposits) to the method of "unified planning, management at different levels, linkage of deposits and loans, with control over the difference."

(6) Internally, the banks should implement enterprise-type management with strict economic accounting. All People's Bank branches and specialized bank branches at or below the provincial level should become independent accounting units and should be eligible for enterprise funds according to the regulations. Interbranch loans should carry a fixed rate of interest.

(7) Financial research organizations should be restored and work in this area strengthened.

(8) Management of bank cadres and personnel
matters should be under the dual leadership
of the Main Office of the People's Bank and
local governments, with the former playing
the primary role. Education and training of
bank cadres should be strengthened.

These recommendations served as a blueprint for
most of the concrete   measures that followed. The
restoration of the ABC came first, on February 23,
1979,[16] followed closely by the establishment of the
General Administration of Exchange Control (GAFX)
and a new higher status for the Bank of China (BOC) on
March 13.[17] In another significant measure, interest
rates on individuals' savings deposits were raised on
April 1, 1979, and three and five year fixed time
deposits with even higher interest rates were made
available.[18] Given the swiftness with which these
policy pronouncements followed the conference of
bank branch directors, it is likely that the meeting
merely ratified decisions already made by higher
levels. The transformation of bank branches into
enterprise-type entities may also have started around
this time. The fact that the State Council circulars
restoring the ABC and changing the status of the BOC
stipulate that all branches of these banks are to
function as independent accounting units strongly
implies that this change had already been made for PBC
branches.[19] Policy changes like granting loans on the
basis of the merit of applicants rather than solely
according to plans could be formally promulgated rather
easily, though genuine implementation is more
difficult.
Other, more consequential reforms were introduced
on an experimental basis in certain parts of the
country. The new decentralized method of credit
planning was tried out in Shaanxi, Hubei, Shanghai,
Fujian, and Tianjin in the second half of 1979.[20]
Later Sichuan, Guangdong, Guangxi, Anhui, Shandong,
Beijing, Liaoning, Jilin, and Heilongjiang were
included in the experimental program.[21] By 1980 the
new scheme was being implemented nationwide.[22] The
PBC started making short- and medium-term equipment
loans in 1979, and by the end of the year the total
value of such loans outstanding was a respectable
Y 792 million (see Table 1). The great increase in
these loans occurred in 1980, however, in part because
of the decision to allocate Y 2 billion in this form to
the light and textile industries. The restoration of
domestic insurance work also took place slowly - it did
not get underway until the beginning of 1980 though it
was planned at a meeting in November 1979.[23]

Major reforms in foreign financing of investment also were promulgated in 1979. A joint venture law came into effect on July 8, 1979,[24] and CITIC went into operation shortly thereafter, though it was officially founded only in October of that year.[25] Quantitatively much more important was the rapid expansion of compensation trade agreements, which had begun in the second half of 1978. These entailed no direct foreign investment and therefore were much simpler from a legal point of view.

Hard currency loans to facilitate production for export were already substantial in 1978. By September of that year over 2,000 plants in China had already received such credits. Total lending of this type was US$9.1 billion in the two years 1979 and 1980.[26] In 1980 the BOC was allowed to make domestic currency loans to finance complementary investment needs of foreign exchange loan recipients; such loans totalled Y 1.136 billion in 1980 and 1981.[27]

Progress was made in providing short-term training courses at which bank cadres could learn professional skills, though this work had started at least as early as 1978.[28] Expansion and improvement of specialized financial institutes of higher education occurred in 1979 as part of a longer-term program.[29] The Chinese Finance Society, an organization to promote research, study, and international academic exchange, was founded at the end of 1979.[30] Similar institutions proliferated in 1980, especially at the provincial level. Other academic research groups were founded and cadre training courses held under the auspices of the Ministry of Finance.[31]

In a significant development, late in 1979 the State Council authorized the People's Construction Bank of China (PCBC) to start funding some state budgeted capital construction projects by means of loans rather than grants.[32] The loans carried an interest rate of 3.0% annually.[33] Their duration is not to exceed 15 years for heavy industrial projects, 10 years for small and miscellaneous projects. Interest on overdue loans or those diverted to a purpose other than that stipulated in the loan contract will be doubled, while early repayment can be rewarded by a lower interest rate. Projects have to meet certain criteria in order to be eligible for loans: (1) their products must be marketable and of good quality; (2) the resources, raw materials, fuel and energy, water resources, and transportation required for production must be ensured; (3) it must be shown with careful calculations that the initial investment can be recovered and the loan repaid on schedule; (4) the land, equipment, materials, and construction manpower in construction projects must have been arranged.[34]

The scope of capital construction loans expanded rapidly; in 1981 nearly Y 5 billion in capital construction loans were granted by the PCBC.[35] In Shanghai in 1981, "all capital construction projects undertaken by enterprises which keep independent accounts and are able to pay debts should be financed by loans extended by construction banks instead of being financed by government funds appropriated gratis."[36] In another significant departure, the PCBC started using its idle deposits to make small, short-term investment loans of its own in 1980.[37]

Whereas 1979 was the year for devising and promulgating major reforms in the banking system, in 1980 these measures were consolidated and implemented on a wider scale. The concerns of economic readjustment came to affect the banking system more and more strongly as 1980 progressed. Preventing an excessive increase in the amount of currency in circulation became an urgent task as inflation became significant. Nevertheless, on balance 1980 was a year of continued and somewhat expanded reforms.

The 1980 nationwide meeting of PBC provincial branch directors, held from late January to early February, added few new items to the agenda prepared by the 1979 conference.[38] The most important change was a new emphasis on withdrawal of currency from circulation. There were three main means of accomplishing this: (1) limiting extension of credit and increasing loan repayments; (2) helping enterprises to produce marketable goods by analyzing market demand; and (3) strictly controlling wage and bonus payments. The other new focus was on improvements in the mode of account settlement. Basically, noncash settlement of transactions between enterprises was to become more flexible and in accordance with the desires of both parties involved. It was also hoped to make crediting and debiting less automatic so that inferior or unmarketable goods would not circulate within the state sector and give paper profits to their producers.

The most important new reform measure in 1980 was the fiscal decentralization already mentioned in the first section of this chapter. Another major new departure was the establishment of trust and investment corporations (domestic) by several provincial PBC branches. Other provincial branches took on trust and investment work themselves by setting up internal departments for this purpose. Trust organizations and departments are true financial intermediaries that mobilize and concentrate scattered financial savings, directing them to investments that foster local economic development. More will be said about trust operations in Chapter 6.

These regional trust and investment corporations
are only one manifestation of a whole set of developments which taken together give China an unorganized
capital market of sorts. Enterprises, government
organizations, collectives, and in some cases individuals can now invest their money in a variety of
productive ventures or joint stock companies. These
operations are especially common in though by no means
limited to rural areas. Though most of these ventures
and companies involve ownership by collective or state-
owned entities as well as individuals, some smaller
operations, particularly in commerce, may be entirely
owned by workers and other individual shareholders. In
addition, opportunities for individuals to invest in
their own small proprietorships have burgeoned; individuals are now even allowed to hire one or two employees. Undertakings invested in at least partly by
private individuals are particularly fascinating, but
joint ventures between state enterprises or between
urban factories and rural collectives are quantitatively far more significant. In these operations
monetary investments are likely to be much less
important than contributions of facilities, equipment,
management skills, labor, space, and raw materials.
Compensation trade, barter agreements, and joint
ventures between provinces are also proliferating.
    Chinese business practices differ from those in
market economies; assets are nontransferable and
therefore no secondary markets exist. The possibility
is always there, however, as is shown by the stringent
prohibition against buying and selling of state
Treasury bonds, even though they are anonymous bearer
securities which could change hands very easily.[39]
Another significant difference is that in China most
people investing in a concern are employees of the unit
that established it, or in the case of rural joint
ventures, residents of the locality. Despite these and
other limitations, China's "newly emerging economic
forms" (of ownership)[40] do provide more free
investment opportunities than have existed in China for
a long time. They also pose a threat to centralized
control over investment.
    One of the ways in which banks can nurture these
new channels for investment flows is by establishing
financial intermediaries like trust and investment
corporations. In other respects the proliferation of
joint ventures and joint stock companies presents more
problems for the banking system than it does opportunities.[42] Most joint ventures raise only enough
capital to cover their fixed investment needs, and
expect bank loans to take care of all their circulating
capital requirements. Urban-rural joint ventures may

try to borrow separately from both the ABC and the PBC,
at differing rates of interest. If a joint venture has
two accounts at different banks, one of the cardinal
rules of socialist banking is broken and bank supervision of financial activities becomes more difficult.
Joint operations are likely to involve various forms of
implicit or explicit trade credit, which also weakens
the ability of banks to impose sanctions.

Another issue that was the subject of debate
during 1980 was bank control of enterprise wage funds.
Limits on bonus payments imposed by banks were very
unpopular with enterprises, which wanted to use their
retained profits for this purpose. Banks found the
responsibility burdensome since it was a constant
source of conflicts. In late 1980 a suggestion was
made that labor and industrial departments be assigned
the task of supervising wage funds.[42] Though the idea
was taken up elsewhere, a State Council decision in
February 1981 required banks to continue and even
strengthen supervision of wages and bonuses.[43] Banks
are probably able to be more independent than labor or
industrial departments in performing this function.

Various new or revived practices were instituted
in certain localities in 1980, which we hear about only
through negative comments or prohibitions. In some
areas discounting of bills of exchange occurred.[44]
Sales on credit and installment purchase arrangements
were common. These helped some units get rid of stockpiles or sell goods in excess supply, like certain
types of machinery, and served as substitutes for price
cuts. In early 1981 credit sales and installment
purchases were strictly limited to long overstocked
commodities, and bank approval was required on a
case-by-case basis. Sanctions were to be imposed
against enterprises that sold goods on credit while
continuing to manufacture them.[45] In 1982, however,
restrictions on trade credit and payment by install-
ments were loosened.

In 1980 suggestions were made to change the way in
which deposits and loans of commercial enterprises were
managed. In most areas past practice had been to
maintain just one bank account for commercial enterprises. All enterprise receipts of funds were
automatically credited against loans outstanding, while
overdrafts up to a planned limit were freely allowed to
cover purchases of goods.[46] The method promoted now
involves separate accounts for loans and deposits.
Enterprises are required to keep a certain amount of
funds on deposit in order to be able to pay normal
expenses. Above the quota level of working capital
requirements, based on the minimum need during the
year, enterprises have to apply for temporary loans,

which are granted on a case-by-case basis only after
careful scrutiny.[47] This method cannot be considered
new; it has been used in at least one city since 1962.
In 1979 and especially in 1980 its use spread to many
localities, though even now it probably is not
universal. Like the changes in modes of account
settlement, reform of commercial credit management is
best viewed as a measure tightening bank control and
trying to prevent purchases of unmarketable commodities
by the commercial system.

The role of the banking system in supporting
readjustment of the Chinese economy was to be that of a
monitor and an instrument rather than a significant
policymaker. Tighter surveillance by banks can provide
political authorities with better guidance as to which
enterprises within specific industries should be shut
down and which capital construction projects should be
cancelled. These decisions are invariably carried out
by means of administrative decrees rather than economic
sanctions such as withholding of credit. Some of the
cutbacks, particularly those in 1981, may have been
made in a haphazard and arbitrary way. On the other
hand, some banks may have continued to grant credit to
enterprises already ordered to shut down, since this
practice was specifically prohibited by a State Council
circular of early 1981.[48]

Interest rates on savings accounts were again
raised in April 1980 (see Table 10). Perhaps more
important, banks were allowed to charge higher penalty
rates for certain types of loans in order to encourage
their prompt liquidation. Interest rates on overdue
loans were raised by 20% (i.e., from 0.42 percent per
month to 0.504 percent per month for industrial and
commercial loans); charges on loans exceeding an
enterprise's agreed-upon quota for circulating funds
and those financing excessive stockpiles of goods were
raised by 30 percent; and interest on loans diverted to
cover cost overruns in capital construction or
renovation projects was raised by 50 percent.[49]

Withdrawal of currency from circulation as an
inflation control measure became a priority task in
late 1980. Several meetings at various levels were
held on this subject between late 1980 and early
1981.[50] In addition to tighter supervision of credit
and wage payments and measures to expand output of
consumer goods and services, more incentives to attract
savings from the population were recommended. In 1981
30,000 more employees to handle savings were to be
hired, and 3,000 additional savings outlets were be set
up within two to three years.[51]

In 1981 readjustment was carried still further,
and a strong attempt was made to balance the budget.

Two key State Council circulars, both promulgated in
February, set the main priorities for the year. The
first was the eight-point decision on keeping a balance
between income and expenditure and rigorously enforcing
financial management, issued on February 3, 1981.[52]
Its main stipulations can be summarized as follows:

(1) The budget should be balanced, and no
     organizations are allowed to spend their
     surpluses from 1980 without approval.
(2) Tax system changes and tax reductions or
     exemptions must be approved by the Ministry
     of Finance, and no enterprises can be added
     to the experimental program replacing profit
     remittances with tax payments, without MOF
     permission.
(3) Similarly, the experimental profit retention
     program for enterprises should not be
     expanded, and profits or depreciation funds
     which should be turned over to the state
     cannot be diverted to any other use.
(4) Large construction projects must be approved
     by the State Council, and the Construction
     Bank has the authority to stop any project
     under construction if it finds irregulari-
     ties.
(5) Excessive stockpiles should be reduced,
     existing enterprises will generally not be
     given additional budget allocations of
     circulating funds, and material supply and
     commercial units may refuse to purchase
     products for which demand is insufficient.
(6) Administrative costs should be cut by 20
     percent in 1981.
(7) The state budget system must be strictly
     implemented.
(8) Financial discipline should be strictly
     enforced, irregularities punished.

A concrete measure adopted by the State Council
on January 16, 1981 made fiscal policy in that year
even more restrictive. For the first time since the
1950s the Chinese Government issued long-term Treasury
bonds.[53] They are supposed to soak up large amounts
of funds in the hands of enterprises, local government
authorities, and other organizations. This excessive
liquidity, of course, is mainly the result of profit
retention schemes and decentralization measures.
Targets for purchases of bonds are set and elaborated
downward through the hierarchy, according to the amount
of excess funds held by a unit. Bond purchases up to
the target are mandatory. The annual interest rate is

4 percent, not compounded even annually, and the
repayment period is ten years. Bonds cannot be bought
or sold. At first sight the interest rate seems very
low, but we must remember that the demand deposits of
enterprises earn only 0.15 percent per month and those
of nonprofit organizations earn no interest at all.[54]
Even the interest rates on deposits at the Tianjin
Trust and Investment Company have been below 4 percent
per year.[55] The long maturity, combined with the
prohibition against any secondary dealings in the
bonds, means that funds will be effectively frozen for
a very long period of time. Involuntary roll-overs in
the future are also a distinct possibility. The 1981
target for total value of bond purchases was Y 4,000
million. Actual sales totalled Y 4.87 billion,
equivalent to over one third of the 1980 budget
shortfall.[56]

In 1981 the central government also felt com-
pelled to exact involuntary loans totalling Y 8 billion from the provinces.[57] But it is important to
note that 1981 Treasury bond sales were designed to
soak up the previous year's surpluses (actually to
finance that part of the budget deficit not offset by
a loan from the PBC to the MOF),[58] while the
involuntary loans were meant to minimize such holdings
in the current year and at the same time reduce
provincial expenditures. Treasury bond issues
continued in 1982, when an estimated Y 4.2 billion
worth were sold. This time about half were sold to
individuals, on a voluntary basis. Treasury bonds
issued to individuals carry an 8 percent annual
interest rate, which makes them competitive with
five-year fixed-term time deposits at banks.[59] In
1983 it is planned to sell another Y 4 billion in
Treasury bonds.

The other main document setting financial
priorities for 1981 was the State Council decision on
strengthening credit management and controlling the
issue of currency, adopted on February 12, 1981. It
also has eight main points:[60]

(1) There should be strict implementation of
credit and currency plans - the central
government has control over currency
issuance, and no organization may force
a bank to extend loans, exempt a loan from
repayment, or divert the funds of rural
credit cooperatives.

(2) Bank credit funds should not be converted
into budgetary appropriations, circulating
funds should not be used for capital

construction, and enterprises must not use bank loans to offset losses or pay wages and bonuses.

(3) Loans should further readjustment objectives, credit to inefficient enterprises should be restricted, and short- and medium-term loans for equipment purchase must be included in the capital construction plan and go through normal approval procedures.

(4) Credit restrictions should be used to reduce excessive stockpiles.

(5) All banking work should be concentrated in banks, no organizations other than banks are allowed to give credit, and trade credit should be limited to measures to promote sales of existing inventories.

(6) Interest rates should be set and changed only by the PBC and subordinate specialized banks.

(7) There should be strict bank supervision of account settlement, cash management, and enterprise payments for wages and bonuses.

(8) Withdrawal of currency from circulation should be promoted.

The many prohibitions in this document tell us something about practices that apparently have continued despite years of efforts to stamp them out. On the surface it is quite restrictive and appears to nullify the effects of several important banking reforms of 1979 and 1980. For instance, point (5) could be interpreted as a prohibition against setting up local trust and investment corporations, though in practice it was applied only to those established by organizations other than banks. Point (1) casts doubt on the new system of decentralized credit management, though it is not clear whether levels of credit and deposits were restricted or merely the difference between them. As in the case of the State Council decree on tightening fiscal management, it is doubtful that many of its provisions were implemented thoroughly or with any great speed.

All in all, the dictates of readjustment overshadowed reforms in 1981, at least in the policy pronouncements of the central government, but there were fewer contradictions between the two in the banking system than elsewhere in the Chinese economy. Economic reforms require strong banks that can give indirect guidance to macro-level economic activity by means of "economic levers." Internal reform of the banking system strives to strengthen local branches in their dealings with clients. Readjustment also

envisions a stronger banking system, but one that will
aggressively further the particular sectoral goals of
the central government. Both reform and readjustment
see the need to make banks independent of the enterprises they serve and local government authorities.
Both require banks to have the ability to monitor the
economy as a whole and the individual units that comprise it. Thus when reforms came back into prominence
in 1982, there was more continuity in banking policies
than in policies concerning other sectors of the
economy.

5
Evaluation of Main Banking Reforms and Policy Changes

Certain of the new policies affecting China's banking system that were surveyed in Chapter 4 deserve more detailed analysis, because of their inherent interest or their implications for the success of China's economic reform package as a whole. The decentralization of China's credit planning and management system potentially could affect the sectoral allocation of credit as well as central authorities' ability to control inflationary pressures. Changes in the structure of interest rates affect the decisions of profit-oriented firms directly as well as the profitability of banking operations. Institutional reforms are crucial in allowing the banking system to assume a meaningful independent role in the economic system. Perhaps the most important change of focus on the part of China's banking system has been its gradual involvement in financial intermediation activities. After a discussion of each of these major reforms, the chapter will end with an evaluation of the degree of success China has achieved in inflation control during the past several years. The crucial area of investment financing will be treated separately in Chapter 6.

DECENTRALIZATION OF THE CREDIT MANAGEMENT SYSTEM

The new method of "unified planning, management at different levels, linkage of deposits and loans, with control over the difference" probably became almost universal in 1980.[1] Because of its potential consequences we will examine the main provisions and implications of this reform in some detail.

The previous system of credit planning was highly centralized; it gave local bank branches very little

freedom of action. Separate targets for deposits and
for different categories of loans were handed down to
bank branches from higher levels. If deposits
exceeded the target the surplus was allocated by and
essentially belonged to the higher-level supervisory
unit. Similarly, if a branch was able to speed up the
turnover on its loans, so that the planned total value
of loans was made with a lower than projected average
or year-end total value of loans outstanding, the loan
funds saved also were controlled by the higher-level
unit. Thus lower-level branches had no incentive to
exert themselves to attract more deposits or economize
on loans.

Under the new system detailed targets for
deposits and loans are still handed down from above.
But instead of being binding they are used to derive a
"difference" which becomes the constraint the branch
must meet. Year-end total planned deposits are added
to any credit funds appropriated from above for the
branch's use, and total planned loans outstanding at
year end are subtracted from this sum. The actual
difference between deposits plus appropriations and
loans at the end of the year must be greater than or
equal to this planned difference. As long as this
condition is not violated, if the bank branch attracts
more deposits it can increase loans by an equal
amount. Provisions are made to take care of seasonal
or unexpected variations in the difference. A bank
branch also is allowed to reallocate loans among the
following categories, as long as the overall target is
met: loans to state industrial enterprises, to
collective industrial enterprises, and to commercial
enterprises, both state-owned and collective.[2]

The new credit planning method is supposed to
stimulate local banks to attract more deposits and
speed up the turnover of loans, for at least two
reasons: (1) increased loans mean higher bank
profits, a portion of which benefit the local branch
and its employees, and (2) making more loans supports
local economic development. Both justifications may
be open to question. The current difference between
loan and deposit interest rates is relatively small;
therefore the profit margin is low. Second, branches
originally could use increased deposits only for
working capital loans, not loans for fixed investment
which are of greater benefit for local economic
development. A more recent report, however, suggests
that now increased deposits can be used in part for
loans to purchase equipment.[3] In any case, the
greater freedom of action and the ability to make
loans outside the dictates of the credit plan must
themselves provide a strong incentive.

Aside from any incentive problems, however, the decentralized mode of credit management may be inflationary. The reason for this is that there is a multiplier effect. A large proportion of a bank loan will be returned to the same bank in the form of deposits. An enterprise may keep part of its loan as a deposit in its own bank account. It may use part of the loan to make purchases from another enterprise, the proceeds being credited to that unit's bank account. Even a portion of that part of the loan used to make wage payments will be returned to the bank in the form of individual savings deposits, based on the marginal propensity to save out of wage income. Thus bank loans in essence create bank deposits. From the viewpoint of a local or provincial bank branch there are only two sources of leakage from this circular flow between loans and deposits: currency that remains in circulation (mostly in the hands of individuals), and enterprise payments to units outside the area of the particular bank branch's jurisdiction. If these did not exist an indefinite expansion of credit would be possible under the new system.

To state this proposition formally, if x is the proportion of a loan that will return to the bank in the form of deposits, then it is easy to show that a unit initial increase in deposits allows the bank to increase its loans by a total of $\frac{1}{1-x}$ units.[4]

Naturally deposits will also increase by the same amount. The induced increase in currency in circulation will be equal to the initial increase in bank deposits, provided this currency is not used to make direct cash purchases outside the locality. If the original rise in deposits resulted from withdrawal of currency from circulation, then that is just balanced by the induced increase, and the net change in currency outstanding is zero. To take a simple example, assume that in one way or another a local bank branch attracts an additional Y 100 in savings deposits by local residents. Assume x = 0.8 and the value of x is left unchanged by the activity that caused the increase in bank deposits, say expansion of the locality's network of savings outlets. In this case the bank branch would be allowed to increase its loans by Y 500, while deposits would increase by Y 400 after the initial rise of Y 100, and currency in circulation would remain unchanged. If the original increase in deposits was the result of an "export" sale to another part of China, then currency in circulation in the particular locality would show an equal increase.

Measures to withdraw cash from the hands of the public other than credit restrictions are likely to increase the value of x, since they tend to increase the proportion of wealth held in the form of savings deposits relative to that held in cash. This increases the size of the multiplier. It is important to note that quantitative restrictions on the amount of currency outstanding will not necessarily prevent the multiplier from operating.

We can obtain a rough idea of the size of the multiplier for China as a whole from the data in Table 1. There are a number of ways of estimating x, but since we are interested in what happens at the margin the best method is to take the increase in deposits in 1980 divided by the increase in loans outstanding during the same period. The resulting approximation of x is about 0.78, giving a credit multiplier of 4.53. If loans and deposits in rural areas are excluded, the estimated value of x increases to 0.842, resulting in a multiplier of 6.32.[5] Though data of comparable quality are not available for earlier years, we can obtain an estimate of the average value of x based on figures for 1957 year-end deposits and loans outstanding. The resulting figures are about 0.73 for x and 3.69 for the multiplier.[6] Of course the value of the multiplier must vary tremendously across regions. For instance, in Liaoning Province the income velocity of currency (1980 national income divided by year-end currency outstanding) was 37.2, more than three times the national figure of 10.5.[7] If bank loans are related to total production at all closely then the value of the multiplier in Liaoning should be far higher than in China as a whole.

The new decentralized system of credit management clearly allows localities to inflate their money supply (in the western sense of the term, including both currency and deposits) well beyond what is called for in the plan. This will increase inflationary pressures, in that the purchasing power that economic units perceive as being available to them will exceed the quantity of goods and materials by a greater margin than before.[8] Controls on the amount of currency in circulation will not dampen the multiplier effect. Active efforts to reduce the amount of currency outstanding for a given level of economic activity will actually increase the value of the multiplier. Direct or indirect quantitative restrictions on bank credit of course will prevent the multiplier from operating, but by their very nature they defeat the purpose of the decentralization measures.

The traditional reasoning of socialist financial
theory that only currency outstanding and not enterprise bank deposits can engender inflationary pressures is faulty. As long as credit is comprehensively
planned and strictly controlled from the top, this
mistaken perception may do relatively little harm.
But when economic reforms put the money supply under
the partial control of local bank branches, neglect of
the monetary nature of credit can cause much more
damage. What is needed is a method of decentralization that gives branches flexibility in deciding on
loans but at the same time allows the center to
maintain some degree of control over the money supply.

CHANGES IN THE STRUCTURE OF INTEREST RATES

Since 1979 China has raised interest rates on
individuals' savings deposits three times (in 1979,
1980, and 1982) and interest rates on loans once (in
1982). Information on interest rate changes is
presented in Tables 10 (for individual deposits) and
11 (for loans). Chinese residents are now allowed to
put their money in fixed-term time deposits with a
maturity of more than one year. Interest is now being
paid on interbranch deposits within the banking system
and on certain other accounts which previously were
interest free. Finally, enterprises, government
departments, and non-profit institutions are now
allowed to put some of their funds in time deposits.
These earn interest at an annual rate of 3.6 percent
for one-year deposits, 4.32 percent for three-year
deposits, and 5.04 percent for five-year deposits.[9]
Interest rates on the most important types of bank
loans also have been raised significantly, after
remaining nearly constant since the late 1950s (with a
slight downward trend) and completely unchanged since
the early 1970s. Moreover, banks are now allowed to
charge extra interest on overdue loans, those financing excessive circulating funds and inventories, and
those diverted to cover capital construction cost
overruns or other unsanctioned activities. Though
interest rates are still set in a unified manner for
the entire country, and changes are made only by
administrative decisions at the highest levels, there
are experiments which let local bank branches charge
up to 20 percent more or less than the official rates
on loans, based on case-by-case evaluations.[10]
Only rarely if ever has the expected real rate of
return on private savings accounts in the People's
Republic of China been negative. With the exception of
the past several years, inflation in terms of official

prices has been negligible since the 1950s. During
the recent bout of inflation the realized real rate of
return may have been slightly negative, but the
expected rate probably remained positive because of
the rise in nominal rates and the difficulty in
forecasting future inflation rates. In any case the
most common feature of "financial repression" in
developing countries, a prolonged and substantial
negative rate of return on private financial savings,
has been absent in China. Three caveats should be
added, however. In the Chinese situation forecasts of
the future availability of consumer goods are probably
more important than forecasts of inflation in determining an individual's choice to save or consume. By
the same token savings may be involuntary in the
context of chronic excess demand for consumer goods at
official prices. Moreover, at various times restrictions on large withdrawals from accounts may have
discouraged financial savings. Finally, the main goal
of the government in encouraging individuals' savings
deposits has been not to mobilize resources to use in
investment but rather to absorb private purchasing
power that might otherwise have exacerbated inflationary pressures in the market for consumer goods.[11]
It is only recently, in the context of the decentralization of credit management, that the role of savings
deposits (and other deposits) in resource mobilization
has begun to receive more attention.

Despite these qualifications, we can conclude that
there are no major problems with the present structure
of interest rates on individuals' savings deposits.
The same cannot be said about the returns on deposits
of organizations and groups. "Economic" units get only
1.8 percent per year for their demand deposits, while
many types of accounts, including those held by
government authorities, mass organizations, Party
Committees, and nonprofit state institutions, earn no
interest at all.[12] The interbank annual rate of
3.24 percent also seems rather low. The interest payments on time deposits enterprises and organizations
are now allowed to receive are probably too low to make
them competitive with other uses of the funds (for
instance, self-financed fixed investments). A general
increase in rates paid on bank deposits of enterprises
and organizations might not attract a great amount of
additional deposits, however, since units are already
required to deposit at the bank all their funds except
for small cash reserves.

On the loan side interest rates may still be too
low in relation to the rates paid on individuals'
deposits, but the 1982 increase in loan rates did much
to close the gap. The bulk of bank loans now carry an

interest rate of 7.2 percent per annum, which is below
what is earned by individual time deposits with a
fixed term of longer than three years. Over three-
quarters of the total value of individuals' savings
deposits consists of fixed-term time deposits.[13]
Moreover, certain agricultural loans carry lower
interest rates than industrial or commercial loans.
Therefore, it may well be that the average rate of
interest on private savings deposits is not far below
the average rate on bank loans, meaning that banks
make only small profits at the margin. They still
make a large profit overall, however, since they pay
no interest or very low interest on the deposits of
enterprises and organizations, which comprised over
68 percent of total domestic deposits at the end of
1980.

Interest payments on loans are only a small frac-
tion of the returns that can be earned from certain
investments. For example, in Chinese industry in 1979
the rate of profit on total assets (fixed assets and
and circulating capital) was 24.2 percent. In
Shanghai the figure was 47.1 percent, in Guizhou
7.7 percent.[14] Because raw materials in China are
underpriced relative to manufactured goods, these
figures may overestimate the true economic rate of
return. Even after the necessary corrections, however, a substantial gap would probably remain. Moreover, marginal rates of return in many sectors are
considerably higher than the average. Interest rates
on loans could probably be raised somewhat without
detracting from the profitability of most investments.

Low interest rates, combined with the fact that
for industrial enterprises most working capital is
financed by state budget appropriations rather than
bank loans, contribute to a somewhat different problem
noted by Chinese scholars. Interest payments are such
a small proportion of enterprise output or profits
that control over credit does not provide banks with
much leverage in guiding the actions of producers.
For instance, interest payments of the Inner Mongolian
Autonomous Region's local industrial enterprises in
1978 amounted to only 1.1 percent of their total
sales, or only 5.5 percent of their "accumulation."
For local commercial enterprises interest payments
were only 2.3 percent of total sales.[15] On the
national level such figures must be derived and therefore are subject to greater error. Nevertheless, a
very rough calculation indicates that for China's
state-owned industrial enterprises, in 1980 interest
payments on loans other than those financing capital
construction amounted to no more than about 0.6 percent of gross output value.[16] It should also be

noted that many loans of circulating funds are never
really repaid but merely rolled over, making repayment
of principal no problem.

All in all, there may be grounds for a modest
further increase in interest rates on bank loans.
However, the authorities may not want to add to the
interest burden on enterprises at a time when the
costs of their raw material inputs are also increasing. There needs to be more variation in interest
rates among various categories of loans and, perhaps,
among regions. At present nearly all loans in urban
areas carry the same 7.2 percent annual interest rate.
Penalty rates could be more severe than they are now,
with gradations, for example, depending on the length
of time a loan is overdue. To make interest payments
a more meaningful part of the average industrial
enterprise's cost structure, changing all working
capital funds into bank loans (the so-called "total-
sum credit" method) would be more effective than any
feasible increase in interest rates. However, this
could be inflationary if budget allocations of bank
credit funds are not increased at the same time.
Otherwise the government might use the extra funds
available from not making working capital appropriations for other, demand-increasing purposes, while at
the same time banks would be forced to grant more
credit to cover enterprise working capital needs. The
interest rates on loans financing fixed investment are
lower than those on circulating capital loans. Nevertheless, credit financing of fixed investment is an
improvement over the previous system of nonrepayable
grants. This reform is still in its early stages, and
future increases in rates are a possibility.

INSTITUTIONAL REFORMS

As was pointed out earlier, the general thrust of
institutional reform of the Chinese banking system is
two-fold: (1) to strengthen and clarify the banking
system's independence vis-a-vis other elements of the
"superstructure" that plans and guides the economy, and
in particular to make a sharp distinction between
fiscal and banking spheres of operation, and (2) to
allow the banking system to deal with enterprises and
lower-level government units from a position of
strength. Much progress has been made toward achieving
the first goal since institutional restoration work
began in 1976, but new problems and bureaucratic
conflicts have arisen, to some extent brought about by
institutional proliferation. As for the second goal,

undeniable achievements have been partly counterbalanced by evidence of continuing widespread enterprise violations of financial regulations. Furthermore, certain features of new banking policies as well
as reforms in other sectors of the economy tend to
undermine bank controls and sanctions.

Jurisdictional ambiguities involving the two main
centers of authority in China's financial system - the
PBC and the Ministry of Finance - are a continuing
problem. The most important of these have to do with
the PBC's attempt to expand the scope of loans it can
make. Previous suggestions that all working capital
funds of enterprises be transformed from budgetary
grants into bank loans now have been dropped. But it
is likely that because of budgetary stringency the
proportion of loan-financed working capital will
continue to increase as it has since the 1950s. In
the case of loans for fixed investment, the PBC can
now grant short- and medium-term loans for equipment
purchases. But loans for major capital construction
projects are handled by the PCBC under the auspices of
the MOF. Innovative new PBC operations like investment-type trust loans, as well as the equipment loans
already mentioned, weaken this monopoly. On the other
hand, loans from the PCBC cover working capital needs
of certain enterprises closely related to construction, and the PCBC has recently begun granting equipment loans of its own. Within the institutional
network supervised by the PBC there are also overlapping jurisdictions. For example, the BOC handles
some domestic currency deposits of export enterprises
and makes domestic currency loans to support export
production.

These and other problems detract from the ability
of the financial system to implement consistent
reforms and weaken bank controls over enterprises by
multiplying the sources to which they can apply for
loans. Moreover, responsibilities for various
operations tend to be divided along bureaucratic
rather than functional lines. What the banking system
has gained from institutional specialization may have
been in part offset by problems of communication and
coordination between different organizations.

In 1979 the PBC gained a considerable degree of
control over personnel matters in its branches.
Appointments, transfers, promotions, and dismissals of
bank cadres are now under the dual leadership of the
PBC and the various localities, with the former playing
the primary role. The number of personnel and wages at
all levels are under the sole control of the PBC.[17]
This may or may not be sufficient to make individual
bank cadres independent from the influence of local

authorities in their decisionmaking. In order to
serve as an independent regulator of the economy the
PBC clearly should have complete and undisputed
control over its internal affairs and particularly
personnel management. That it has not yet entirely
achieved this is testimony to the continuing strength
of local interests. Moreover, in trying to gain
complete control over its branches the PBC is
attacking the dual leadership concept, which has been
dominant in China since the 1950s.

In terms of substantive policy the debate over
whether local (meaning provincial-level) bank branches
should serve the needs of local development or safe-
guard the interests of the central government still
continues. In late 1980 various articles were urging
banks to play a greater role in fostering local
construction.[18] The 1981 tightening of readjustment
may have dampened this somewhat. On the other hand,
recent developments like the prospective domestic and
international bond issues by the Fujian Investment and
Enterprise Company[19] show that regional autonomy in
making major financial decisions continues to be
significant. China probably would benefit from having
separate financial institutions to support local
development and to implement national policies. But
the PBC's control over economic activity in the state
sector derives entirely from its direct supervision of
credit, cash, and noncash transactions of enterprises.
As yet few if any effective indirect macroeconomic
control mechanisms have been developed, so if the PBC
becomes removed from its direct contact with grassroots
economic units it loses whatever ability it may have
had to direct the economy.

The extent of influence bank branches actually
exercise over their clients is difficult to ascertain.
The past several years have witnessed great efforts to
improve financial discipline, and there have been
numerous reports of successful bank intervention to
alter enterprise behavior. Unquestionably considerable
improvements have been made. The increased number of
reports on lax financial work or even malfeasance are
in part a sign of more careful monitoring by financial
institutions rather than an indication of actual growth
in such activities.

Bank sanctions are now backed up to some extent by
the threat of eventual shutdown of an enterprise,
though that of course is a high-level political decision. During 1979 over 3,000 state enterprises in
China were closed, suspended, merged with other units,
or shifted to other lines of production. They comprised about 3.6 percent of the total number of such
units.[20] The greater effectiveness of financial

sanctions, however, may increase incentives for enterprises to misrepresent their financial position in order to show more profits. This only aggravates the perennial problem of manipulation of accounting categories in order to use more funds for investment, which may have become worse in the past several years. Diversion of bank loans for working capital to fixed investment has been a common form of irregularity, one that is difficult to monitor. Joint ventures of various kinds open up a whole new realm for actions that bypass traditional bank supervision. Inter-enterprise trade credit has also grown, legitimized to some extent by the need for favorable terms to sell off unwanted inventories. As credit restrictions have tightened it is quite possible that involuntary trade credit has grown rapidly.

FINANCIAL INTERMEDIATION

The view of banks as financial intermediaries that mobilize the scattered savings of society and channel them to productive uses is a significant departure from the traditional approach in centrally planned econom-ies, which does not see enterprise bank deposits as true savings and advocates attracting private savings mainly for inflation control purposes. One aspect of Chinese banks' new role is the explicit link between the deposits local branches attract and additional loans they are allowed to make, discussed earlier in this chapter. The ability of banks to mobilize savings in this way, however, is sharply limited by the types of securities they can offer, namely regular bank deposits with low rates of return. On the other side the only investments banks can make are ordinary loans carrying the burden of all the stipulations and restrictions of state credit policy.

The other avenue by which banks can become or create financial intermediaries appears to be more promising. In Chinese discussions it is referred to as "trust work," though this term also includes advisory services and other activities. Trust operations can be handled either by a specialized independent corporation set up by the local bank or by a trust department within the bank itself.[21] Trust work was proposed by a high-level meeting of PBC branch directors sometime around the middle of 1980, and expanded rapidly there-after. However, trust and investment corporations other than those established by banks were specifically prohibited by Premier Zhao Ziyang in a speech in early 1982.[22]

The main sources of funds for trust operations
are the temporary surpluses of state enterprises,
collective enterprises, industrial management
departments, local governments, mass organizations,
military units, schools, and other nonprofit entities,
as well as loans from the PBC, accumulated profits,
and in some cases funds from local offices of the
People's Insurance Company of China.[23] The ways in
which trust and investment organizations can attract
savings are slightly less restricted than those of the
banks themselves. Fixed term deposits of one, three,
and five years are permitted, with escalating rates of
return which should be set somewhere between the
interest rates on enterprise deposits and those on
individual savings deposits. The Tianjin Trust and
Investment Corporation (TTIC) set the following rates
in 1980: 0.18 percent per month for six-month
fixed-term deposits; 0.21 percent for one-year term,
0.24 percent for 2-year term, and 0.30 percent for
three-year term.[24] Trust organizations and departments also accept deposits earmarked for investment in
a particular locality or a particular unit. This
feature attracts government entities and other organizations interested in promoting investment and
determining its direction more than merely earning a
return on their idle funds.

There are essentially four ways in which the
funds gathered can be utilized: regular loans, earmarked loans, investments made on behalf of depositors, and investment-type loans. The main recipients
of such investments are the various joint ventures and
newly established limited liability joint stock companies that have proliferated recently. The TTIC
charged the following rates in 1980: 0.51 percent per
month on one-year loans, 0.57 percent for two-year
loans, and 0.66 percent for three-year loans.[25]
Earmarked loans and investments are made with funds
deposited for a specific purpose (it is not precisely
clear if and how risks are shared in the case of the
latter). Investment-type loans involve deferred
repayments from the profits of the project supported,
once it is under way.

By the end of 1980 PBC branches had established a
total of 241 organizations dealing with trust work.
In 1981 the number further grew to 383. Their balance
of trust deposits reached Y 940 million at the end of
1980 and Y 1.99 billion by the end of 1981. Loans and
investments of all kinds outstanding totalled Y 910
million at the end of 1980 and Y 1.57 billion at the
end of 1981.[26] Though these aggregates are still
quite small in relation to total deposits and loans of
banks, they have been growing very rapidly.

As in the case of financial intermediation by banks themselves, the main obstacle in trust work is probably the limited variety of assets and low rates of return offered to savers, though this is belied by the statistics just cited. Given the high rewards of direct investment in various types of productive projects, organizations which are free to do so could make much more profit in this way. Some units like schools, military detachments, and other nonprofit entities are probably not allowed to invest directly in joint ventures. They also earn no interest on their bank deposits, so the rates offered by trust organizations might appear more attractive. The main supporters of trust work, however, are likely to be local governments and possibly the local bank branches themselves, which want to stimulate and direct local economic development. Local governments and bank branches may deposit funds in trust institutions either to escape the restrictions imposed by state policy on their own loans or to avoid depositing their surplus funds with higher-level bank branches. On the investment side trust organizations make few, if any, long-term loans or investments. The primary securities they purchase (loans or shares) are not marketable or transferable. The interest rates on loans should make them attractive to borrowers, especially those who have no access to regular bank loans or investment allocations from the budget.

In the Chinese context financial intermediation of the type just described may hinder attempts to strengthen bank supervision and promote economic stability. The greater part of the savings supposedly being mobilized may be involuntary. It is questionable whether unspent budgetary allocations of entities like schools and mass organizations should be used for investment purposes. What probably happens in the process of financial intermediation in China is that scattered deposits representing scattered, relatively small amounts of unsatisfied excess demand are brought together and concentrated in such a way that demand for investment goods is stimulated, exacerbating disequilibrium in this sector and contributing to the so-called "overextension of the capital construction front." In the case of trust operations, where relatively few of the depositors are individuals, it cannot even be claimed that disequilibrium in markets for consumer goods is being ameliorated. Financial intermediation as it has developed so far in China is probably too restricted to provide the significant benefits normally associated with such activity, while at the same time it increases demand in a sector of the economy where disequilibrium is already acute.

INFLATION CONTROL

Since 1979 China has experienced significant
inflation in retail prices. The index of retail
prices rose by 2 percent in 1979, 6 percent in 1980,
and 2.4 percent in 1981. The cost of living of
workers and staff rose by 1.9 percent in 1979,
7.5 percent in 1980, and 2.3 percent in 1981.[27] For
certain categories of goods price rises were much
sharper. For example, prices of nonstaple foodstuffs
reportedly rose by 32.1 percent between 1978 and
1981.[28] Though quite moderate compared to international inflation rates, these price increases followed
virtual stagnation in price indexes during most of the
1970s.

Raw materials and other inputs have also been
subjected to partially repressed inflation. This
manifests itself in persistent shortages accompanied
by rising inventories. Firms become reluctant to sell
commodities in short supply at official prices.
Furthermore, they know they will have difficulty using
the monetary proceeds of any sales to obtain supplies
that they need. This leads to excessive holdings of
material reserves against future contingencies. Side
payments in both monetary and nonmonetary form are
commonly needed to complete transactions, and barter
is sometimes resorted to.

Chinese sources attribute the current inflation
mainly to large budget deficits, which result in
excessive currency issuance by the PBC.[29] Deficits can
be overt, like those in 1979 and 1980, or they can be
covert, meaning that they do not show up in the
accounts but result in excessive currency issuance just
the same. Some examples of the latter are: production
of substandard or unmarketable goods, which are sold to
commercial departments and thus generate profits and
tax revenue, even though the commodities concerned are
carried as inventories until they are written off
or sold at a loss; use of bank loans by enterprises to
pay profits and taxes to the state; insufficient
budgetary allocations of working capital, which mean
enterprises must ask for bank loans in order to
maintain their normal operations; diversion of circulating funds to capital construction; and taut
planning which overestimates revenues and underesti-
mates expenditures.[30] If these factors are taken
into consideration the already significant budget
deficits in 1979 and 1980 would be even larger.

The main causes of the overt deficits of these
years are measures on both the revenue and the
expenditure sides to improve living standards and
material incentives (higher wages and more bonuses in

industry, higher purchase prices in agriculture), combined with difficulties in controlling expenditures on fixed investment. The government also significantly reduced its share in certain revenues, notably profits of state enterprises, to stimulate their production and efficient operation. The fiscal decentralization had a similar effect.

Two other factors now operating in the Chinese situation may be at least as significant causes of inflation as budget deficits. Both are results of economic reforms. Increased stress on profits means that enterprises and various other units now have a much greater incentive to manipulate prices. It is generally far easier to increase profits in the short run by charging higher prices than by improving management or expanding markets for output (as long as there is insufficient competition in the economy). Because of extensive legal restrictions, price manipulation can take many forms, some overt, others concealed. The great publicity accorded to mass campaigns on price inspection and administrative circulars prohibiting various kinds of price manipulation provide ample testimony that such practices are widespread.

Secondly, various reforms have increased the funds in the hands of enterprises and localities. There is at least the presumption that retained funds can be used for purposes chosen by their owners, within fairly broad limits. Thus an implicit corollary of the reforms is an increase in the "moneyness" of bank deposits, at least as perceived by their owners. To the extent that bank deposits are less restricted as to disbursement and use, they contribute more to demand for commodities and therefore to inflationary pressures. Despite a rapid 29.3 percent rise in currency outstanding during 1980, nearly 80 percent of the total increase in money supply (currency plus deposits) in that year was in the form of bank deposits.

Money supply can be increased by either budget deficits or bank credit. In 1980 the realized budget deficit was Y 12.75 billion (Table 7). This was dwarfed by the Y 39.7 billion rise in the sum of currency and deposits (Table 1). Even if the money created directly by the budget deficit is subtracted, the rate of increase in money supply created by the banking system in 1980 was 17.2 percent, considerably higher than what was called for by the growth of the economy in that year. Assume very roughly that the 6.9 percent increase in real national income, 7.2 percent increase in total industrial and agricultural output value, and 8.7 percent increase in total industrial output value that occurred in 1980[31]

would have allowed a 10 percent noninflationary
increase in money supply. Then inflationary money
creation by the banking system totalled over Y 11.5
billion, making its contribution to inflationary
pressures approximately equal to that of the budget
deficit. These calculation have no claim to accuracy,
but they do show that the banking system itself can be
as important as the budget deficit in generating
inflation through money creation.[32] We must
remember, however, that much of the increase in credit
(and therefore deposits) may be forced on the banks as
a result of various fiscal policies.

Chinese methods of fighting inflation appear not
to have changed greatly over the years, despite significant modifications in China's economic system,
economic structure, and relative price structure.
Attention is focussed on currency rather than
deposits. The main means by which currency can be
withdrawn from circulation are: (1) quantitative
controls on credit; (2) efforts to increase the
financial savings of individuals; (3) expansion in the
production of light industrial consumer goods and the
sales of services; (4) increases in state purchases of
agricultural products from rural areas which can be
sold to the urban population: (5) strict controls over
cash transactions and reserves in the state sector;
and (6) a balanced budget, with any surplus frozen.
Of these measures only the first and last reduce bank
deposits as well as currency outstanding. Moreover,
even in the current situation it is not clear that
rigid quantitative restrictions on credit are being
imposed. More likely efforts are being made to
terminate outstanding loans that are being used for
"incorrect" purposes (like capital construction or
excess stockpiles), as well as making certain that new
loans granted meet the standard criteria. The other
main means of preventing inflation is strict administrative controls on prices, which do not attack
underlying causes.

Clearly measures that do no more than reduce the
amount of currency outstanding will have only limited
success in moderating inflationary pressures. In
particular, mere transformation of money in the hands
of the public from cash into savings deposits is not
likely to moderate their demand for commodities significantly. It is also doubtful that increasing state
purchases of agricultural products moderates inflationary pressures in the present situation. In the
1950s low agricultural purchase prices and relatively
high (though not market-clearing) retail prices for
urban consumers meant that state agricultural purchases and subsequent retail sales in either processed

or unprocessed form probably resulted in a net withdrawal of individuals' purchasing power from circulation.[33] Since then the average price paid by the
state for farm products has increased, because of
gradual shifts in categories from compulsory purchases
at the lowest prices to nominally optional purchases at
higher prices and more recently significant hikes in
the procurement prices themselves. As a result many
commercial units handling agricultural purchases suffer
losses which must be made up for by subsidies from the
government. This means that the process now causes
more currency to be released into circulation in rural
areas than is absorbed in urban areas, resulting in a
net inflationary impact.

There is no question, however, that the combination of a tight budget, strict credit controls,
aggressive price monitoring, and expansion of consumer
goods supplies can reduce inflationary pressures.
This is apparent in the much lower increase in the
retail price index in 1981. Chronic excess demand for
investment goods may be more difficult to control.
Credit controls may help somewhat, but the most
important methods being used are administrative
restrictions on various kinds of investment expenditures (likely to be evaded) and involuntary loans and
bond purchases by local governments and other organizations with surplus funds.

6
Investment Financing

Financing of investment in China at first sight appears to be a relatively straightforward process centered around the state budget. This impression of simplicity is deceptive for a number of reasons: (1) Problems of definition make transformation of Chinese accounting categories into those relevant for our analysis difficult. (2) Large amounts of investment expenditures are financed by extrabudgetary funds, a heterogeneous category including items ranging from regular fiscal revenues to depreciation allowances retained at various levels to retained profits of enterprises. (3) Self-financing of investment is common, especially in agriculture, while in industry significant amounts of investment may have been routinely listed as expenditures on current production. (4) Budgetary allocations for circulating capital and for bank credit funds are difficult to interpret: do they affect physical investment in inventories or working capital at all, or are they an accounting device used primarily to ease inflationary pressures? (5) The sources of funds for credit-financed investments present other problems as well – the aggregate level of credit to some extent determines the level of deposits, so bank loans partially "create" their own source of financing. (6) How are financial savings related to the real savings of society? In an only partially monetized economy how should involuntary savings be treated? Transformation of the excess demand for consumption goods represented by private financial savings into added demand for investment goods by means of bank credit does not necessarily imply a reallocation of real resources from consumption to investment. (7) Should unspent budgetary allocations temporarily in the bank accounts of various units be regarded as savings? In a command

economy framework these deposits mean little in terms
of real purchasing power because they must be spent
for specific purposes and can be used as means of
payment only when accompanied by extensive
documentation.

These and other questions may not have answers,
but they do show the need for caution in making quantitative estimates or qualitative judgements about
investment financing in China. Nevertheless, a few
salient points emerge. Economic returns on aggregate
investment are low and have been declining since the
mid-1960s. Part of the reason for this is certainly
the mode of financing, in the case of both fixed
investment and accumulation of circulating capital.
Important changes in the past three years may have
given economic units more incentive to invest in
projects with the highest financial returns. On the
macro level, however, these reforms may have lowered
the efficiency of investment because of the lack of
connection between financial resources and supplies of
materials as well as distortions in the structure of
relative prices. Lack of coordination between
regional investment programs remains a serious problem, one which may have been exacerbated by decentralization and a new emphasis on profits by the
localities. Just as important as the effect of
reforms on the composition of investment demand has
been their impact on the level of investment demand:
Demand has been stimulated by growth of retained
discretionary funds of lower-level units and greater
availability of bank credit to finance fixed investment. The resulting increase in excess investment
demand has in turn reduced the efficiency of
investment.

We will first look at the main sources of investment funds and then evaluate some of the means by
which savings are transformed into investment expenditures. Finally we will consider evidence on the
efficiency of investment in China.

INDIVIDUAL SAVINGS

Private financial savings in China rose steeply
in 1979-82 (see Table 12). With the exception of
extrabudgetary funds they have been the fastest growing source of investment financing. The net increase
in individuals' savings deposits during 1980 was
equivalent to 29 percent of net new credit extended by
banks and credits cooperatives that year. In 1981 the
proportion reached 34 percent. Since over three-
quarters of savings are in fixed-term time deposits,

they may to a large extent represent at least a
temporary withdrawal of the population's purchasing
power from circulation. This contrasts with the bank
accounts of enterprises and organizations, which for
the most part technically are demand deposits. Unfortunately we have no information on the percentage of
individual savings in time deposits of different
maturities.

Table 13 shows that there is a huge quantitative
gap between urban and rural savings both in per-capita
and in aggregate terms. This gap has continued to
widen in absolute terms despite the fact that the rate
of increase of rural deposits has exceeded that of
urban deposits in recent years. At the end of 1980
per capita urban deposits exceeded those in rural
areas by over 1,400 percent, at the end of 1981 by
nearly 1,200 percent. This overstates the propor-
tional gap in individual holdings of financial wealth,
since the rural population has a much higher ratio of
currency holdings to bank deposits than do urban
residents.

The private financial savings rate has climbed
steadily since the mid-1970s, as can be seen from
Tables 14-16. Some of the proxies used for income
may be unreliable, but all three tables show the same
unmistakable trend. Perhaps the most meaningful
relationship is the ratio of incremental urban savings
to the total wage bill. This rose from 2.5 percent in
1977 to over 10 percent in 1982 (Table 15). The ratio
of private financial savings to national income for
the country as a whole has also risen sharply from
1 percent in 1978 to over 3 percent in 1980 and 1981
(Table 14). It is now much higher than at any other
time since 1949. The estimates of the rural savings
rate should be considered unreliable, since the per
capita rural income figures used (from sample surveys)
appear to be biased upward by a considerable margin.
Nevertheless, the sharp upward trend in 1978-81 is
noteworthy.

In considering individual savings as a source of
financing for investment the question naturally arises
as to whether these savings are voluntary or not. Do
these savings result from the free choice of individuals or are they dictated by shortages of consumer
goods? Available evidence indicates that at least
urban savings may well be largely voluntary, since the
growth of urban incomes appears not to have far out-
stripped the growth in supplies of consumer goods. In
1978 the nominal value of urban retail sales rose by
8.8 percent, while the total wage bill grew by 10.5
percent. In 1979 urban retail sales increased by
9 percent, while nominal wages rose by 13.5 percent.

In 1980 the corresponding figures were 16.6 percent and 19.5 percent, respectively, in 1981 8 percent and 6.2 percent. All in all, between 1977 and 1981 nominal wages rose at an average annual rate of 12.3 percent, urban retail sales by 10.5 percent.[1] Though nominal wages did grow slightly faster than retail sales during this period, this can be explained at least in part by measures that increased the attractiveness of holding savings. Even if disequilibrium got worse in 1979 and 1980, restrictions on the growth of nominal wages in 1981 must have ameliorated the situation.

At rural free markets and, more important, at urban markets where peasants can freely sell their products, transactions have steadily increased and prices until 1981 were declining (in 1981 there was a moderate rise of 6.6 percent).[2] These trends are consistent with the assertion that urban savings to a large extent are voluntary. Otherwise excess consumer purchasing power would have been directed to these free markets, resulting in sharply rising prices. At the very least, disequilibrium in the urban market for consumer goods is not so severe that people prefer to buy high-priced agricultural goods rather than saving in the hope of obtaining a consumer durable in the future. Large-scale involuntary savings are compatible with the existence of functioning free markets for farm products only under one of two conditions: (1) people are satiated in terms of their diet, so that increasing the amount or improving the quality of the food they consume does not improve their welfare; or (2) prices are so high that people prefer to save despite uncertain supplies in the "official" consumer goods market. Only the second alternative is a real possibility in China. The two main factors involved, however, are free market prices and the probability of obtaining a desired consumer durable. The lower the former, the higher the latter must be in order for people to choose saving over immediate consumption of food. Stagnant free market prices for food combined with increased savings would imply that the probability of obtaining other consumer goods has risen or at least not decreased.

This reasoning suggests that the urban population is saving in order to purchase consumer durables. In fact, increased supplies of consumer durables and the prospect of further increases in the future may have actually stimulated urban savings. Given their high prices and the lack of consumer credit in the economy, months or more likely years of saving are required in order to buy items like bicycles and TV sets. Even three or five year fixed-term deposits may be considered as vehicles for saving to purchase consumer durables.

In rural areas people may also be saving to purchase consumer durables, but a considerable amount of anecdotal evidence suggests that supplies still fall far short of demand.[3] Nominal rural incomes rose by an estimated 71 percent between 1978 and 1981, while retail sales grew by only 63 percent.[4] Cash income must have risen even faster than total income. These rough figures combined with other, qualitative evidence do suggest that rural savings may to a considerable extent be forced by shortages of consumer goods. In urban areas, by contrast, most consumer complaints concern overt and covert price hikes rather than lack of availability per se. This also tends to support the assertion that urban savings to a large extent are voluntary.

On the positive side numerous measures have been taken to attract more savings deposits, including substantial increases in interest rates, expansion of the savings network to provide better services, and innovations like lottery savings accounts in some localities. Perhaps the most significant change is simply enforcement of standard principles on private savings: "voluntary deposit, free withdrawal, interest payments, and protection of the anonymity of savers."[5] Neglect of these policies in the past undoubtedly made bank deposits unattractive as a form of saving, especially for those with large sums of money.

BANK DEPOSITS OF ORGANIZATIONS

Deposits belonging to units other than individuals and rural collectives form the largest "source of funds" of the banking system. Excluding government budgetary accounts, at the end of 1980 they accounted for over 65 percent of domestic deposits in state banks. In 1980 the net increase in bank deposits of enterprises, government departments and organizations, and capital construction funds was equivalent to more than 50 percent of the net increase in state bank credit. Only a part of these funds can be considered legitimate sources of investment financing. In the first place they are all nominally demand deposits, though many administrative restrictions may be placed on their use. Secondly, unspent budgetary allocations should not be viewed as real savings of society, especially when the budget is in deficit. Given severe disequilibria between demand and supply for capital goods, especially raw materials, many of these

deposits clearly represent involuntary savings. As
one Chinese scholar states:

> Banks are holding some deposits that are false.
> When government deficits get really big, funds
> financed by deficits for the purpose of capital
> construction and funds earmarked for subsidizing
> purchases and sales that are not immediately used
> are temporarily deposited in the bank. The banks
> then face the situation of having "false deposits
> and real loans."[6]

A case in point is deposits of capital construction funds, which rose sharply in every year for which
data is available and increased by 75 percent between
1979 and 1981 (see Table 1). These represent mainly
funds already earmarked for use in capital construction investment but not yet spent. Thus their
increase reflects restrictions imposed on investment
projects rather than any growth in the savings of
society. The banking system should not consider
increases in deposits like capital construction funds
a sound basis for further expanding loans to finance
fixed investment.

Some deposits come from extrabudgetary funds of
various kinds, which will be discussed separately.
Though they can be allocated directly for investment
purposes by their owners, it is questionable whether
they should be considered a valid source for bank
credit. This is particularly true if such funds are
"frozen"; it would defeat the purpose of China's
current readjustment policies if localities were
prevented from spending funds for certain purposes but
banks could turn around and extend credit, using the
"frozen" deposits as the source of funds.

In present circumstances, then, it is inappropriate to view bank deposits of organizations and
groups in the same way as individuals' savings. But
this may well be what the new decentralized credit
management system does, in effect. Trust companies
also may exacerbate problems and inflationary
pressures by accepting deposits from organizations
and groups, which they transform into additional
demand for investment goods.

FOREIGN FINANCING

This is a source of investment funds which has
received increasing attention in the past several
years. Though policy measures have stressed means of

attracting foreign investment without incurring foreign debts, the latter have been quantitatively very
important. Capital construction appropriations in the
state budget financed by foreign loans came to Y 7.09
billion in 1979, Y 7.3 billion in 1980, Y 7.308 billion in 1981, and an estimated Y 5 billion in 1982.
Foreign loans accounted for the following proportions
of budgetary capital construction appropriations:
13.8 percent in 1979, 17.4 percent in 1980, 22.1 percent in 1981, and 16.5 percent in 1982 (Table 7). By
all indications foreign financing will continue to
play an important role in China's budgetary capital
construction investment in the future, but perhaps the
peak reached in 1980-81 will not be equalled.

China places great hopes on "new" forms of
foreign trade and investment which minimize foreign
exchange requirements and result in no foreign debt.
Results so far have been mixed. Equity joint ventures
involving direct foreign investment undoubtedly have
been the most visible. By March 1981 twenty-two such
joint ventures were operational, with a total investment of more than US$210 million.[7] According to a
different source over $170 million consisted of
foreign investment.[8] Another 360 "contractual" joint
ventures with a total investment of US$500 million had
been started by early 1981. In contrast to equity
joint ventures, income of the parties is determined by
firm comitments rather than investment shares:

> In the contractual joint venture, (the) two sides
> agree to firm commitments. The foreign business-
> men usually provide funds, equipment and tech-
> niques, while China provides sites, labor,
> management personnel, raw materials and other
> services... each side is allotted a certain ratio
> of products, sales volume and profits. In the
> light of the agreement, China is responsible for
> operation of the venture. The operating period
> is usually shorter than for equity joint
> ventures.

Finally, four agreements on offshore oil drilling
had been signed as of early 1981, with an investment
of over US$800 million. All told, the investment
figure has reached US$1.65 billion. Of this total
about US$1.2-1.3 billion consists of foreign invest-
ment.[9] We have no figures on annual increases in
foreign investment, but they must have been quite low
in terms of actual investment rather than contract
signatures. Joint ventures have considerable potential for the future as legal complexities get ironed
out. Significant involvement of foreign companies in

offshore oil drilling could easily make direct foreign
investment the largest component of foreign investment
financing.

In 1980 a total of three large and 350 small and
medium compensation trade agreements were reached.
The imports of foreign equipment involved totalled
US$187 million.[10] Other modes of trade like pro-
cessing and assembly of imported materials also may
entail imports of equipment, but the total value must
be very small. All in all, compensation trade, processing and assembly deals, countertrade, and various
forms of barter are more important because of the
foreign exchange they generate or save than for the
small amount of foreign investment they stimulate.
Recent critiques of compensation trade in the Chinese
press show some disillusionment with this type of
activity.[11]

It is highly unlikely that internationally-
floated bonds will ever become a major source of
investment funds for China, barring major policy
changes by the central government. However, some provinces may already have started issuing domestic
currency bonds whose principal is repayable in foreign
currency, to attract investment from Hong Kong residents and overseas Chinese.[12] Though at present no
quantitative information is available, these bonds may
grow in importance if they become sanctioned by the
central government.

Since joining the IMF and the World Bank in 1980,
China has begun to borrow considerable amounts from
the former and started several investment projects
financed by the latter. Even before these milestones
China had already begun to utilize some foreign aid.
Foreign aid and concessionary loans of various sorts
will become more important since China has cut back
further on its short-term borrowing, which carried
interest charges the Chinese view as prohibitive.

Viewing the whole issue of foreign financing of
Chinese investment more broadly, it is clear that
foreign trade itself or more specifically exports are
the most important means of paying for imports of
investment goods. This section has focussed more
narrowly on nontrade investment financing, but it
should be recognized that Chinese exports will always
be the crucial determinant of the amount of investment
China can make through importation of capital goods.[13]

THE STATE BUDGET

Budgetary data provide a detailed breakdown of
China's revenues and expenditures (Tables 6 and 7).

The large budget deficits in 1979 and 1980 resulted in an increase in money supply, since they were financed by overdrafts drawn from the PBC. Thus a portion of investment expenditures in both years was funded by money creation. On the PBC ledger, of course, the additional credit extended to the state treasury was offset in large part by the new deposits thereby created. The small budget deficits of 1981 and 1982 resulted in much less money creation.

Though the state budget remains by far China's single most important source of investment funds, its relative importance has declined steadily since 1978, as can be seen from Table 17. In 1978 the national budget financed over 82 percent of total capital construction investment; by 1981 the figure had dropped to under 49 percent, and in 1982 it may have continued to decrease.[14] A significant chunk of China's national investment has thus been rather quickly removed from the supervision of the government budget. In 1981 central authorities tried to regain control over investment expenditures by a variety of methods, including administrative restrictions imposed on investment projects and absorption of extrabudgetary funds by means of involuntary loans and Treasury bonds. The latter are a substitute for money creation in financing budget deficits. The 1981 Treasury bond target of between Y 4 and Y 5 billion was designed just to offset the difference between the planned and actual budget deficit in 1980. Starting in 1982, proceeds from Treasury bond sales were included in the budgetary accounts as ordinary revenue.

Involuntary loans by the provinces to the central government are designed to force the former to reduce their expenditures. These loans were targeted at Y 8 billion in 1981, exactly the size of the projected central government deficit vis-a-vis the localities.[15] Shanxi Province alone was required to loan Y 319 million to the state in 1981, in addition to purchasing Y 120 million worth of Treasury bonds. The loan funds reportedly were to come from cutting capital construction investment by Y 186.73 million and administrative expenditure by Y 132.27 million.[16]

EXTRABUDGETARY FUNDS

We have no systematic quantitative data on extrabudgetary funds that would permit a detailed analysis. Various sources offer differing estimates of their total value. Therefore this discussion will be limited to a list of the main sources of extrabudgetary

funds, their history, and some comments on prospects
for the future.
Perhaps the best place to start is Donnithorne's
early (1967) account:

> The sources of those funds are many and
> diverse, but they include major regular
> revenues and not just casual items. Profits
> retained by enterprises and their controlling
> ministries (including provincial and lower
> level counterparts of these ministries) have
> formed the largest single item. Other items
> include local surtaxes to industrial and
> commercial tax, to agricultural tax and to
> urban public utility charges; the road tax,
> local budgetary surpluses carried down from
> previous years, enterprises' major repair
> funds, labor protection and welfare funds,
> irrigation charges, income from the labor of
> students and employees of schools and other
> organizations, school fees, fees for admittance
> to parks, museums and sports grounds, income
> from water supplies, rents, the sale of night-
> soil, the hiring of halls and of vehicles and
> fees for the certification of weights and
> measures... As well as these officially acknow-
> ledged revenues, hints are thrown out about
> others that are illicit, such as excess
> retained profits, and profits that remain
> uncollected because local financial departments
> failed to make contact with enterprises trans-
> ferred to local control. Other sources of
> extrabudgetary revenue, while not illicit were
> unofficial, such as 'voluntary' contributions
> which some hsien (counties) are reported at one
> time to have levied from agricultural producer
> cooperatives or the similar contributions
> demanded from individual officials on occasion
> in some places.[17]

Retained profits can be divided into those kept
by the enterprises themselves as a result of current
experiments and those retained by industrial management departments under the system of enterprise funds,
50 percent of which are supposed to be spent on the
enterprises that earned the profits.[18] In addition
industrial bureaus and local authorities handle the
after-tax profits of large collective enterprises.[19]
Depreciation funds are also retained in part by
various enterprises and their managing departments.
Many of the items mentioned by Donnithorne must be
relatively insignificant as sources of revenue.

Undoubtedly the most important sources of extrabudgetary funds are depreciation funds retained at
various levels below that of the central government,
profits retained by the enterprises themselves, their
managing departments, and in some cases local authorities, and the proceeds of special local and regional
government taxes taken as a whole.

Both the size and the composition of extrabudgetary funds have changed considerably since the
First Five Year Plan period. Most of the information
we have available is on investment expenditures from
extrabudgetary funds, not extrabudgetary revenues per
se. Investment out of extrabudgetary funds amounted
to Y 465 million in 1957 and about Y 5 billion in
1958, a jump of nearly ten times. As Donnithorne
notes, the chief reason for this precipitous rise was
the institution of a profit retention system.[20] The
demise of this system in 1962 probably resulted in a
decline in extrabudgetary funds. During the Cultural
Revolution depreciation funds were placed at the
disposal of enterprises or their immediate superiors
rather than being allocated by the center.[21] This
undoubtedly caused an increase in extrabudgetary
funds. By 1976 38 percent of gross fixed investment
in China's state-owned enterprises was provided by
extrabudgetary funds. This figure may be representa-
tive of the situation in the early and mid-1970s. By
1979 the proportion had risen slightly to 40 percent,
despite the fact that a portion of depreciation funds
had again been placed under central control. In 1979
the experimental profit retention program, under which
enterprises were allowed to keep a larger proportion
of their depreciation funds as well as profits, began
in earnest. In 1980 extrabudgetary expenditures rose
to comprise 55 percent of gross fixed investment in
state-owned units.[22] This is undoubtedly less than
the proportion of China's total fixed investment
accounted for by extrabudgetary funds, since these are
the primary, often the only source of financing for
investment in or by collectively-owned enterprises.

Somewhat surprisingly in view of the 1981 emphasis
on retrenchment, the central authorities have not taken
steps to decrease the amount of extrabudgetary funds
significantly. Instead the government has tried to
neutralize them by various means. Treasury bonds
absorb a considerable proportion of extrabudgetary
funds. The funds have not been confiscated, only
frozen for a period of time. On the expenditure side
all investment spending is now supposedly subject to
strict controls, including replacement investment and
technological innovation projects undertaken by the
enterprises themselves, which previously had not been

included in plans. Thus extrabudgetary funds continue
to accrue to various units, but their usefulness may
now be more limited.

Several salient points emerge from this brief
consideration of extrabudgetary sources of investment
financing:

(1)   Extrabudgetary funds are quantitatively
       very important and have financed an increas-
       ing proportion of China's fixed investment
       in the past several years (well over half in
       1980).

(2)   Their future role is in doubt, since they
       prevent the center from controlling one of
       the most important variables in the economy
       - the rate of investment.

(3)   The greater proportion of extrabudgetary
       resources are at least nominally subject to
       central control. The amount of depreciation
       funds retained at various levels is deter-
       mined by national policy, as are the terms
       of profit retention schemes.

In this light the failure of central authorities
to reduce the flow of extrabudgetary funds at their
source is hard to explain. For instance, rather than
instituting ad-hoc measures like issuance of Treasury
bonds or administrative restrictions on investment
projects, it would have been relatively easy for the
central government to make reductions in profit retention rates and in the proportion of depreciation funds
kept by lower-level units. In part the government may
not have wanted to rescind measures that expanded the
scope for independent decisionmaking by lower-level
units so soon after they were implemented. But in
fact this is being done anyway by the restrictions on
investment projects. A more likely explanation is
that the center may not have the ability directly to
retract popular policies that place more funds in the
hands of lower levels. If this is true it testifies
to the strength of the localities vis-a-vis the
central government.

This completes our discussion of the main sources
of funds for investment. We now turn to the means by
which savings are transformed into investments, which
is a distinct process from the generation of savings
in the first place. The budgetary intermediation
mechanism and the banking system have already been
treated extensively elsewhere. Self financing and
direct investment will receive some attention. The

only nonbank financial intermediaries are the PICC and
the trust and investment corporations, both of which
have already been described in other sections.

SELF FINANCING

A widespread mode of transforming savings into
investments, especially if its scope is broadened to
include investments made in subordinate factories by
industrial bureaus and local authorities, is self
financing. Its primary source of funds is extrabudgetary funds. In addition, some self-financed
investment may be listed as current expenditures on a
firm's books. This means that it is funded in part by
the enterprise's own profits (some or all of which
otherwise would have gone to the government), in part
by unpaid taxes.

In an environment with a well-functioning capital
market, self financing need not result in inefficient
investment patterns, since the funds used have a high
private opportunity cost. In China until recently
there were few alternative investment opportunities,
and bank accounts paid little or no interest, so it is
quite likely that many projects with low returns were
invested in. Now the alternative of direct investment
in a joint venture of one kind or another does exist
to some extent, raising opportunity costs. But
undoubtedly these opportunities vary widely from firm
to firm, depending on the many factors which determine
how easy it is to form a joint venture. Thus direct
investment, whatever other merits it may have, is no
substitute for a high-yield financial asset that
enterprises can put their surplus funds into. Such an
asset (or group of assets) need not be the product of
a true credit market. The PBC could simply make
special accounts with longer maturities and high
interest rates available to enterprises on a voluntary
basis. This would curb inefficient self-financed
investments if their cause was indeed lack of attractive alternative uses for surplus funds. Despite the
factors which would tend to cause self-financed
investments to be inefficient, these investments are
probably no more inefficient than budget-financed or
even credit-financed investments.

Though there are no statistics on the aggregate
volume of self-financed investment in the Chinese
economy, we do have information on some of its
components. Nearly all depreciation funds retained by
the enterprises themselves and the greater part of
those kept by lower-level management units probably go
into this form of investment. To a lesser extent the

same is true for retained profits. These two totalled
at least Y 16 billion in 1980, and must have paid for
the lion's share of self-financed investment. By 1982
the total amount of profits retained in various ways
by the entire state sector had reached Y 17 billion;
with retained depreciation funds added the total must
have been double the 1980 figure.[23]

DIRECT INVESTMENT

Unlike self financing this is largely a new
phenomenon, though direct investment may also have
been used to some extent in the 1960s readjustment
period. It probably does not account for a large
proportion of China's total investment at present, but
expansion in recent years has been very rapid.
Foreign and domestic direct investment operate under
very different rules. The former is carefully monitored and heavily taxed, while the latter at least
until 1981 was subject to few if any formal regulations. Direct investment should also be distinguished
from various forms of amalgamation, which fall under
the general title "specialization and coordination."
Here enterprises become parts of larger entities which
may restrict their independence in various ways, as
opposed to investing in a new concern which they
jointly control with other partners. On the other
side, investments by industrial bureaus and local
governments in "their" enterprises should be considered a form of self financing rather than direct
investment.
Direct investments are made in bodies variously
termed "joint ventures," "joint operations," "joint-
stock companies," etc. The investors share in the
profits according to the value of their investments.
So far there is no evidence that shares are transferable in terms of ownership, though transferability
may not have been specifically prohibited. Procedures
are not uniform, and the details of investment valua-
tion (including setting a price on land, facilities,
or other nonmonetary contributions), management
control, source of material inputs, and control over
the output of the joint operation, are decided by
negotiations on a case-by-case basis. Though we have
few reports of unsuccessful joint ventures, there
seems no reason why those that fail cannot be
dissolved. The employees of such operations are often
members of one of the partners, and presumably could
simply return to their original jobs in the event of a
shutdown.

Investment shares are generally denominated in monetary terms, presumably at official prices where those are applicable. Most reports stress the different nonmonetary contributions of the investors, however. Access to raw materials is a particularly important prerequisite, though facilities, labor, equipment, and management expertise are also necessary ingredients. On the output side division of the operation's products among the various partners may be more important than their respective profit shares. First we will look at a few of the quantitatively more significant operations, those that include urban state-owned enterprises and rural collectives as partners, then we will consider joint ventures including investments by individuals. Finally, interregional cooperation will be briefly discussed.

One much-praised example of urban-rural joint ventures is the Shanghai Dazhihe Woolen Mill, under the joint management of the Wool and Jute Fabric Company of Shanghai's Textile Industrial Bureau and two communes in Shanghai's suburbs.[24] Its equipment consists of 5,200 obsolete British-style woolen textile spindles supplied by the urban partner; the plant was constructed by the two rural communes on land belonging to them. Most of the labor force consists of members of the two communes, some of whom were sent to one of Shanghai's urban woolen textile mills for training. Management and technical personnel were drawn from the urban side of the partnership. The jointly-managed mill should be very profitable if it can get adequate supplies of raw materials. Investment totalled about Y 4.32 million, 55 percent from the Wool and Jute Company and 45 percent from the communes. Land is not included in the figure for the rural share; instead the joint venture pays the communes rent on an annual basis for the right to use their land. Apparently the rental rate was determined by the value of the crops that could have been grown on the acreage converted to industrial use. Annual output value of the plant is estimated at over Y 30 million, of which after-tax profits total Y 4 million, implying a payback period of just over a year.

An example of a somewhat different type of urban-rural industrial joint venture is the Beijing Yinghai Bicycle Parts Plant, established by the Beijing Main Bicycle Plant and the Yinghai Branch of the Nanjiao State Farm.[25] Whereas in the Shanghai concern discussed above the original motive was to find some productive use for aging textile machinery that had been replaced, in this example the main commodity traded was space. The bicycle plant, like

many of China's light industrial enterprises, was
located in very cramped quarters and could not further
expand production on its own. At the same time the
agricultural machinery plant in the state farm had
insufficient business, perhaps as a result of
restructuring in this sector. In a very sensible
arrangement the latter was partially redesigned to
produce parts and do electroplating so that bicycle
production could be expanded.

The Tianjin Second Light Industry Bureau (which
manages collective enterprises producing low-tech-
nology or handicraft products like leather goods,
carpets, suitcases, etc.) was involved in twelve
urban-rural joint ventures as of the middle of 1980,
most of them producing carpets or clothing.

> These enterprises are under the unified
> management of the industrial side in the
> fields of the supply of raw materials, pro-
> duction, and marketing, and the industrial
> side also provides equipment, technology, and
> a part of the floating capital. The agri-
> cultural side provides factory buildings and
> manpower. The [joint] enterprises undertake
> independent accounting, make themselves
> responsible for profit and loss, pay taxes
> locally, retain 5 percent of their profits as
> enterprises' funds, and divide equally the
> remainder between the two sides.[26]

Here again the goal is expansion of production in the
face of capacity constraints, but the relatively
simple characteristics of the production process allow
the technology to be transferred in its entirety to
the joint venture.

Many joint ventures include individual shareholders, a sharper departure from the prereform system
than those involving only organizations. One example
is a factory to produce sake and soy sauce and to
operate a flour mill set up by a commune in Shandong
Province. It issued 1,250 shares of its stock at a
par value of Y 100; they were sold both to various
collectives and to individuals. The shareholders meet
four times annually to decide on management policy.
60 percent of the corporation's profit is distributed
to shareholders, 20 percent is retained for expansion,
and 20 percent goes to the commune that founded
it.[27] Another instance occurred in Sichuan
Province, where an integrated silk enterprise set up
by a county had insufficient capital, despite
investment by the state and communes and brigades in
the area. Therefore investments by individuals were

solicited, with the added attraction that those
investing more than Y 500 could make arrangements for
qualified relatives to work at the enterprise. Within
a few days 426 individuals had applied to purchase
shares worth a total of Y 213,000. Eventually only
105 people were actually allowed to invest.[28]
In Fuyang Municipality, Anhui Province, local
authorities issued shares in order to raise funds to
develop light industry and handicrafts. These were
bought by factories, stores, urban neighborhoods,
rural communes and brigades, individual workers, and
peasants; within a few days Y 7.2 million worth were
sold. The method by which investors are recompensed
is particularly interesting: "The investors may
receive a dividend or secure employment for a relative
or friend at the factory. Those who wish neither of
these may receive an interest 10 percent above that
given on savings accounts."[29] This shows a lack of
differentiation between purchases of shares and
extensions of loans, which is common in these new
business dealings.
In some cases employees at a plant invest in
certain operations of that factory:

> ... the Mudanjiang Coal Machinery Plant
> set up a limited liability furniture company
> by using unused machinery and work time
> normally frittered away after the regular
> work had been completed. Seventy percent of
> the net profit goes to the company's accumu-
> lation fund, 5 percent is put aside as reserves
> and the remaining 25 percent covers dividends
> for directors, investors and workers and staff
> members.[30]

There are no national figures on domestic joint
ventures. In Shanghai Municipality at the end of 1980,
there were 287 such joint enterprises, with a total
investment of Y 410 million.[31] Quantitatively much
more important are the various types of interprovincial
cooperation, particularly compensation trade. Like
international compensation trade agreements these
technically do not involve equity direct investment.
The province providing equipment implicitly makes a
loan to the other partner, which is later repaid with
part of the new output produced with the equipment.
Sometimes the loan is purely financial, but part of
the agreement stipulates that a certain proportion of
the resulting output must go to the party that made
the loan.[32] In some cases the contract even calls
for a certain amount of commodities to be turned over

to the provider of the equipment in advance (presumably using existing production facilities).[33] The
main motivation behind many of these deals is securing
raw materials. Because of current shortages strong
inducements often must be offered to the material-pro-
ducing areas, including sometimes a portion of the
final output made with the raw materials supplied.
Other forms of interregional trade, including barter
and processing and assembly of materials, are also
generally oriented toward establishing secure sources
of supply.

Despite the great diversity of concrete methods
and arrangements used in direct investment, there are
some common features: (1) Most joint ventures and
interregional trade agreements involve China's new
priority sectors - light and textile industries,
agriculture, and animal husbandry; indeed, this may be
one of the means by which these sectors achieved such
impressive output growth. (2) Direct investment
generally involves a certain amount of technology
transfer, though as in the case of international
arrangements of this sort the benefits to the
"backward" partner sometimes are open to question.
(3) Returns are high, often involving payback periods
of less than a year.[34] This is partly the result of
China's structure of relative prices, partly of past
neglect of these sectors. (4) Investments are usually
made in kind, not money, though monetary values are
used to determine profit shares in most cases.

It is likely that various forms of direct investment will continue to flourish. The gains from trade
of this sort are often very great, since in the past
very little adjustment in factor endowments took
place, especially in sectors that did not receive much
state investment. Joint ventures may be an efficient
substitute for additional government appropriations or
construction of entirely new facilities. The fact that
many operations are oriented toward obtaining supplies
of raw materials means that they will continue to have
strong support from the industrial areas that need
these inputs.

EFFICIENCY OF INVESTMENT

The efficacy of working capital investment has
already been discussed (see Chapter 3), since it is
relevant to a discussion of past policies and performance in China's banking system. A major new
departure in China's current financial reforms is
credit financing of fixed investment. Reforms have
affected financing of fixed investment in other ways

as well. Therefore it is appropriate to evaluate the efficiency of fixed investment in this chapter. We will look briefly at historical trends.

Chinese reports confirm a sharp increase in the amount of new investment associated with a given increase in national income. During the First Five Year Plan period (1953-1957), the amount of investment required to generate a Y 1 increase in national income was Y 1.68; by the Fourth Five Year Plan period (1971-1975) this figure had risen to Y 3.76, more than doubling.[35] Even in 1976-1978 there was only a slight improvement to Y 3.20. Scattered sector-specific data also show a general decrease in the efficiency of investment. Construction costs rose and lead-times grew considerably; the ratio of increased fixed assets to capital construction expenditures declined, from 83.7 percent during the First Five Year Plan period to 59.5 percent in the Third Five Year Plan period and 61.4 percent in the Fourth Five Year Plan period.[36]

More important than any decreasing efficiency or increasing costs of construction was lack of compre-hensive planning of different investment projects. This has caused the utilization rate of China's fixed assets to be low, because of lack of raw materials, energy, and necessary complementary investments, especially in infrastructure. According to one Chinese source, of total fixed assets added between 1952 and 1978, less than two-thirds could really be utilized effectively.[37] Though these and other statements like the assertion that 30 percent of China's industrial production capacity cannot be used because of electricity shortages should not be taken as careful estimates, they do provide some indication of the magnitude of the problem. Returns on invest-ment in China are low not primarily because of inefficiency in the construction stage, but rather as a result of poor planning that results in unbalanced growth of capacity in different sectors. An excessive aggregate investment rate also tends to decrease efficiency. It should be noted that greater attention to profitability of investments may make construction itself more efficient while exacerbating problems caused by the lack of comprehensive planning and coordination. Relative prices are skewed to make manufacturing in general and light industrial produc-tion in particular overly profitable. Thus use of the profitability criterion would cause excessive investment in this sector. Raw materials-producing areas would have an incentive to hold back supplies and construct small, inefficient plants in their own territories in order to capture some of the manufac-turing profits.

Though the banking system clearly played some role in causing low and declining returns on investment in China, it has not been the primary factor in this. Until recently most fixed investment was not credit financed. Moreover banks were often prevented from performing supervisory functions that might have identified and prevented the worst forms of waste. In the prereform situation only planning could attempt to minimize intersectoral imbalances, ensure that capacity did not outrun input supplies, and make careful preparation and evaluation of projects. With the implementation of economic reforms that enhance the role of the banking system in financing fixed investment, the situation has changed to some extent. China's banks now can take part of the credit for any improvements in the efficiency of investment, but at the same time they bear some of the responsibility for any deterioration in the efficiency of investment that may have occurred.

7
Eastern European Banking Reforms: The Lessons for China

China differs from the countries of Eastern
Europe in many ways. The most salient differences are
apparent from even the most superficial observation.
China dwarfs the whole of Eastern Europe in size and
population - many Chinese provinces are larger than
most Eastern European countries. China is an underdeveloped country with a low standard of living; the
nations of Eastern Europe vary greatly, but with the
possible exception of Albania they are all richer and
more developed than China. These Eastern European
countries (except for Yugoslavia and Alabania) have
close econimic ties with each other and with the
Soviet Union; the great preponderance of China's
foreign trade is conducted with non-Communist partners. This difference in international economic
orientation is partly related to size, partly a result
of geopolitical considerations. Eastern Europe is to
varying degrees politically subservient to the USSR
(again with the exception of Yugoslavia and Albania).
China on the other hand has not been a part of the
Soviet bloc for two decades and conducts an independent foreign policy. In terms of natural resources
and particularly energy Eastern Europe is relatively
poor, China fairly well endowed, though not in per
capita terms. The former is a large net importer of
energy, the latter an exporter. Finally there are
cultural and historical differences which defy brief
explanation.

Nevertheless, meaningful comparative analysis of
economic reform in China and Eastern Europe is
possible, for a number of reasons. With the partial
exception of Yugoslavia all Eastern European countries
have centrally planned socialist economies, as does
China. Direct state intervention in the economic

activities of micro-level units is pervasive in both
China and Eastern Europe. All the countries considered here had their economic systems transformed in
the years after World War II. In all cases the model
followed was that of the Soviet Union, though variations soon emerged to accommodate differences in
initial conditions and the goals of policymakers.
Despite the difference in level of economic development between Eastern Europe and China, both the former
countries and the latter espoused the goal of "catch-
ing up" with the advanced capitalist countries by
means of rapid growth and massive structural changes.
Modes of thinking about the economy in these countries
started out from a similar foundation of Marxism-
Leninism combined with conventional wisdom learned
from practical experience in the Soviet Union. Many
of the difficulties that Eastern European countries
hoped to solve through economic reforms in the 1960s
and that China is wrestling with now are natural
consequences of the imposition of central planning and
state ownership on any economy. Thus economic reforms
in China and Eastern Europe can be viewed as variations on the theme of response to harmful, unwanted
side effects of a centrally planned economic system.
Though to some extent differing responses were the
result of differences in objective conditions,
conscious, relatively freely made policy decisions
also played an important role in determining outcomes.
Therefore different paths of economic reform can be
compared not merely as responses to different situa-
tions but also as "experiments" with at least some
similarity in initial conditions - the centrally
planned economic management system imposed on Eastern
Europe by the USSR and consciously emulated in China.
    In a more positive vein, comparison between
economic reforms in Eastern Europe and those presently
being attempted in China is a useful exercise because
it may enable the latter to avoid some of the many
pitfalls encountered by the former. There are abundant
signs that reform-oriented Chinese economists have
studied the Eastern European experience and try to
apply what they have learned in discussing China's own
economic policies. We will see, however, that in
certain areas China appears to be repeating the errors
that Eastern European countries made in devising or
implementing economic reform packages. Sometimes China
has avoided problems that turned out to be the nemesis
of economic reforms in some Eastern European countries,
not because decisionmakers learned from the past but
simply as a result of perceived constraints on policy
that prevented an erroneous direction from being taken.
So at least in terms of concrete actions there is

considerable room for improvement by China in learning
and applying lessons from the Eastern European
experience.

The scope of this discussion generally will be
limited to Eastern European banking policies and
reforms, though broader assessments may be included
where relevant. There will be no attempt comprehensively to survey developments; several scholarly
publications already do that.[1] In addition some
useful country studies have appeared.[2] Instead we
will try to distill some meaningful lessons that may
be of practical import for China. The main focus will
be on those countries that implemented the most drastic reforms: Yugoslavia starting from the early 1950s
and Hungary after the New Economic Mechanism was
introduced in January 1968. But other Eastern
European countries, where banking reforms were
subsequently rescinded (German Democratic Republic,
Bulgaria), made impossible by political events
(Czechoslovakia), eroded away over a period of years
(Poland), or not seriously considered in the first
place (Romania), may provide negative lessons that
will prove just as useful as the more positive
experience of Yugoslavia and Hungary. Developments in
the Soviet banking system will also be considered when
they shed light on China's situation.

RELATIONSHIP BETWEEN BANKING REFORMS AND
REFORMS IN THE REST OF THE ECONOMY

Experience in Eastern Europe has shown that banking reforms cannot be too far out of step with reforms
in the rest of the economic system; otherwise they may
be ineffective or even harmful. If banking reforms go
too much farther than economic reforms elsewhere they
will be meaningless. On the other hand an unreformed
banking system will slow the progress of overall
economic reform.

Except for Yugoslavia, the two countries that
envisioned (and briefly implemented) the most radical
reform of the banking system were the German Democratic
Republic and Bulgaria, where there were no significant,
lasting reforms in the rest of the economic system.
The basic goal of banking reforms in both countries was
the transformation of bank branches from supervisory
organs representing the interests of the state into
profit-oriented firms that deal with their clients in
a businesslike manner on the basis of equality.[3]
Each branch would become a commercial bank responsible
for its own profits, while the head office would
become a separate bank of banks, with note-issuing and

refinancing functions similar to those of the central
bank in a market economy. In the case of Bulgaria,
the state bank was expected to use reserve requirements as well as discount rates to influence the
actions of the commercial banks. The new reforms were
implemented on January 1, 1968 in the German
Democratic Republic and on April 1, 1969 in Bulgaria.
The transformed banking system did not outlast the
first problems it encountered. As Zwass notes:

> It soon became obvious that in a planned economy
> where there is no natural interplay between
> supply and demand for credits or between credits
> and the interest rate, and where all indicators
> must be regulated administratively, planned, and
> set centrally, a market-type banking system makes
> no economic sense. There was no apparent way to
> reconcile the refinancing and interest mechanisms
> and interest rates with the binding target
> figures of the economic plan.[4]

Bulgaria reverted to its old system in 1971, East
Germany in 1974.

The institutional scenario envisioned by the
GDR-Bulgarian banking reforms is not too different
from some of the proposals of Chinese economists.[5]
Moreover decentralized credit management and independent accounting by bank branches, both of which are
policies actually being implemented in China, together
include the essence of the reforms in the two Eastern
European countries without making the specific institutional bifurcation. Though in China bank branches
still have plan targets, these are not binding if
extra deposits can be attracted. In one sense the
Chinese reforms are even more radical because they do
not give the head office of the PBC any instruments
like discount rates or reserve requirements with which
to affect branch decisions. On the other hand the
institutional arrangement gives the center the
opportunity to retain at least some degree of control
by means of direct administrative orders.

It is not clear what real effect the Chinese
measures have had so far on concrete actions at the
branch level, but the events in the GDR and Bulgaria
suggest that caution is warranted. Even though
economy-wide reforms have already made some progress,
they may not yet have gone far enough to make a
profit-oriented, market-type banking system meaningful.

The experience of Yugoslavia in the 1950s shows
that lack of reform in the banking system can cause
problems if the rest of the economy has been radically
transformed. The first approach to banking reforms by

the Yugoslav authorities was based on the premise that
bank supervision should replace other control instruments being discarded as self-management was instituted: "It seemed advisable that decentralization in the
market for goods and services be accompanied by strict
centralization in the financial sphere."[6] The incon-
gruities between self-management in commodity markets
and a state monopoly in finance soon became apparent,
leading to decentralization and functional specialization. But administrative decentralization alone did
not ameliorate many of the banking system's
deficiencies:

> The National Bank offices were inefficient and
> unimaginative, engaged in distributing the
> planned increase in credits and executing the
> decisions of the head office. Communal banks
> fell under the complete control of local
> authorities, which often made it impossible to
> conduct a sound business policy of profitable
> and safe investments. The federal government
> often directly interfered with the banking
> business by immobilizing certain kinds of
> deposits...[7]

In the mid-1960s Yugoslavia wholeheartedly reformed its
banking system; at present despite many problems it is
far more consonant with the institutional structure of
the economy than the banking system of the 1950s and
early 1960s.

FINANCING OF FIXED INVESTMENT

        Nearly all the countries of Eastern Europe,
including even the Soviet Union to some extent, have
increased the proportion of total fixed investment
financed by bank credits and enterprises' own funds
(primarily retained profits), at the expense of budgetary allocations. This is a response to the widely
perceived problems believed to be caused by the latter
method of investment financing: excessive demand for
"free" investment resources by enterprises, proliferation of construction starts to lay claim for future
investment funds, long gestation periods for projects,
and low returns on the investments made. The change
in investment financing from fiscal appropriations to
interest-bearing loans need not be accompanied by any
significant reforms in the banking system itself. The
flow of funds to investment projects becomes loans,
while the return flow of profits is reduced, replaced
by repayments of principal and interest on loans.

Unfortunately credit financing of investment has proven no panacea. Too many projects still get started, construction times remain long, returns low. Even in Hungary these problems remain, despite carefully thought out and at least partially implemented complementary reforms designed to make the shift to credit financing effective. The reasons for continuing difficulties vary from country to country, but some of them are probably inherent in the economic system rather than the specific way in which credit financing was instituted. Interest rates are often too low: the 3 percent annual charge on capital construction loans in China is just one example. Profits may not be as important an incentive to enterprises as physical output, in which case they will demand more investment projects in order to expand output despite lack of profitability. As long as bankruptcy is no real threat this demand is infinite for all practical purposes.[8] Allowing firms to make investments from their own retained profits may be especially harmful if their opportunity cost is low - if they cannot be lent to banks or other financial institutions at high rates of return. Even if profits do matter to enterprises, they may be able to avoid interest costs by passing them on to consumers through higher prices. The relatively small size of Eastern European countries and their protected markets mean that many industries have only one or a few firms, making monopolistic price setting a serious threat if reforms have proceeded that far. In China the national market is larger, but regional and even local "administrative protectionism" appears to be the rule, creating tiny markets which in many cases may not approach the minimum efficient scale of a single firm in size. On the other hand enterprises in China still play an extremely restricted role in determining prices for their output.

Developments in Eastern Europe suggest that there are a number of preconditions which must be met before the shift to credit financing can result in significant improvements in the efficiency of investment. Enterprises must have significant decisionmaking power and should be influenced by profit and cost considerations. Interest rates must be high enough that interest payments become a significant part of costs. Prices should be exogenous from the point of view of the individual firm. Bankruptcy must be a real threat to loss-making enterprises. In China some of these conditions are not met at all, others only partially. Moreover sectoral overinvestment is undoubtedly encouraged by China's distorted price structure. This suggests that the new Chinese innovation of capital construction loans may not fully realize its intended benefits.

EXCESSIVE ENTERPRISE LIQUIDITY

The ability of banks to influence enterprise actions depends crucially on the liquidity at the disposal of the latter. Two aspects of economic reforms tend to increase both the amount of money owned by enterprises and more important their freedom to use it for their own purposes: (1) expanded decisionmaking authority for basic-level units, the keystone of economic reform, means nothing if it does not extend to at least some portion of an enterprise's financial resources (potential or actual); (2) in practice profit retention schemes and other financial incentives almost invariably result in a net increase in funds at the disposal of enterprises, even if they were not designed to do so.

Excessive levels of enterprise liquidity mean less need for bank loans, so the credit sanction becomes less threatening. More important, enterprise money holdings contribute to excessive investment demand. In theory it should be possible to allow firms to put their funds into long-maturity high-return financial assets issued by the government, thereby enhancing bank controls (the enterprises no longer have a large reserve of funds to fall back on) and choking off excessive investment demand. In practice authorities have rarely been able to resist using coercive methods to neutralize enterprise funds: taking direct control of projects financed with enterprise funds (the USSR), freezing of various enterprise bank accounts (Yugoslavia in the 1950s), and involuntary bond purchases (China), among others. Needless to say the effect on incentives may be harmful.

One practical solution to the problem is suggested by the Hungarian device of charging relatively high rates of interest on loans for circulating capital and allowing enterprises to choose between credit financing and self financing.[9] This had the effect of increasing the proportion of working capital financed by the enterprises themselves and may also have played some role in the lower growth rate of inventories in the late 1960s and early 1970s as compared with the early 1960s.[10]

China has recognized the harmful effects of excessive liquidity in the possession of enterprises. Authorities have attempted to neutralize the effect on investment demand by strict direct controls over

116

investment projects as well as mandatory bond sales
and (in the case of local governments) involuntary
loans. These methods have been only partially
successful.

CREDIT RESTRICTIONS AND TRADE CREDIT

The goal of credit restrictions imposed by the
state bank in a centrally planned economy is generally
not to reduce the aggregate level of economic activity
per se; such restrictions usually have the more
limited objective of controlling inventories and
promoting more efficient use of circulating funds by
enterprises. In some cases the authorities may also
hope to reduce the outflow of currency into circulation and thereby dampen inflationary pressures.
Credit restrictions have generally proven ineffective
in attaining these objectives, since enterprises
respond with an increase in involuntary trade credit
that cascades and permeates the economy. This soon
becomes a worse problem than those that the initial
restrictive policy was meant to address. Ad-hoc
devices to alleviate the situation like multilateral
clearing procedures are ponderous and unwieldy. In
the end the authorities generally respond with an
easing of bank credit that reduces the amount of trade
credit but negates the purpose of the original
measures.
In the USSR trade credit and "claims of payments
difficulties" became serious problems in the years
following World War II.[11] Innocent suppliers could
not meet their own obligations when their customers
defaulted or delayed payment. To alleviate the
situation an increasing number of Bureaux of Mutual
Settlements were set up to undertake multilateral
clearing of interenterprise debts. By 1954 their
number reached about 700, up from 150 at the end of
the war. In 1954, 45 percent of all payments were
made by means of multilateral clearing of debts.
Starting in that year credit was eased and the
importance of involuntary trade credit gradually
decreased. In Poland there were two periods of tight
credit policy: 1951-1955 and 1958-1961. In both cases
the result was a predictable increase in involuntary
interenterprise trade credit. Bank measures to offset
debts by no means solved the problem. Again the only
real improvement came when credit was eased, obviating
the necessity for defaults on payments.
Burgeoning involuntary trade credit in the face
of tight monetary policy has been a pervasive phenomenon in Yugoslavia, and has been the subject of

scholarly attention.[12] Delays and defaults in
payments have been shown to be a rational response to
tight credit, considering Yugoslavia's inflationary
environment. Once again a key part of the story is
the virtual impossibility of bankruptcy for major
nonprivate enterprises in Yugoslavia. As a result
debts almost never become a threat to continued firm
operations. Self-management does not carry with it
assumption of ultimate managerial risks by workers.
In Yugoslavia trade credit has become a restricted
means of payment that is widely used, an ironic
development because one of the major achievements of
economic reforms in that country was near-elimination
of administrative controls over enterprise bank
accounts. Since the scope of multilateral clearing
(apparently undertaken by the enterprises themselves)
is relatively narrow, it is really an elaborate form
of barter, with all the associated inefficiencies.[13]
In addition trade credit can frustrate the goals of
bank supervision:

> During easy money perinds trade credit funnels
> bank credit from firms which have more or less
> unlimited access to bank loans to borrowers who
> are rationed out of part of the bank credit they
> seek ... During tight money periods the same
> rules for trade credit and extension prevail,
> but borrowers attempt to obtain additional
> temporary credit by defaulting or by post-
> poning payment on outstanding trade bills
> while negotiating new ones.[14]

In deciding whether or not to impose a restrictive credit policy the authorities face unpalatable
alternatives. Enterprises will circumvent restrictions by defaulting on and delaying payments, which
results in an increase in the aggregate level of
involuntary trade credit in the economy. This makes
it more difficult for banks to evaluate the financial
performance of enterprises and allows excessive
inventory accumulation to continue. An easy credit
policy allows the banks to monitor a higher proportion
of total credit in the economy but does not prevent
inefficiencies in the use of credit funds.
    In China, scattered references to what appears to
be transferable trade credit [15] may indicate that this
phenomenon is even more pervasive than it is in Eastern
Europe. Indeed, trade credit is now explicitly sanctioned to promote sales of goods for which demand is
insufficient or to sell off unwanted excess inventories. On the other hand, in the present readjustment
period the threat of shutdown must influence the

behavior of at least some enterprises. The possibility of shutdown varies tremendously with the size of
an enterprise, its technology, and the sector,
industry, or region it operates in. Even so, in the
current situation there may be real constraints on the
amount of involuntary trade credit an enterprise can
obtain. In that case the restrictive lending policies
now being applied in China may be more effective than
those previously instituted in Eastern Europe. We do
not have a great deal of information about the role
trade credit has played in the Chinese economy in the
past, though it must have been important at various
times. On the other hand there is ample evidence that
"involuntary bank credit," mainly in the form of
overdue loans, is pervasive.

FINANCING OF CIRCULATING CAPITAL

Experience has shown that the distinctions among
various kinds of working capital that are part of the
traditional Soviet model are arbitrary and ineffective
in preventing excessive inventory accumulation. In
practice the level of a firm's inventories is more
important in determining the amount of credit it
receives than the norms or quotas for different kinds
of circulating funds that it is assigned.

Among the various improvements tried out
Hungary's seems the most promising and may well be
applicable to China. Enterprises are no longer given
a quota of circulating capital that they are entitled
to. Instead they choose the amount of circulating
funds they prefer and can meet their needs by any
combination of bank credit and their own funds.
Interest rates on loans are high, so "Credit is not
taken if it is more profitable for the enterprise to
use its own funds."[16] The proportion of credit in
circulating funds in Hungary fell by almost half in
the years since the New Economic Mechanism was
introduced. There is also evidence that at least in
the late 1960s and early 1970s the growth of inventories slowed significantly.[17]

INSTITUTIONAL REFORM

Except in Yugoslavia the general trend in Eastern
European and Soviet banking has been one of institutional and functional consolidation. Taking the Soviet
Union as an example, in 1959 the specialized agricultural bank and the communal and housing bank were
absorbed by the state bank, while investment financing

in industry and state-owned agricultural units came to
be handled by a single investment bank. In 1963 the
previously separate network of savings banks was put
under the supervision of the state bank. At present
the USSR has an institutionally simple banking system
consisting of only three organizations: the state
bank, the investment bank, and the bank for foreign
trade.[18] In other countries consolidation has gone
even further: investment banks were abolished and
their functions transferred to state banks in
Bulgaria, Czechoslovakia, Hungary, and Poland, while
even in Yugoslavia the distinction between banks
extending short-term credit and those financing
long-term investments has disappeared in practice.[19]

    In China, as we have seen, institutional proli-
feration has been the rule during the past five years.
The size and importance of the agricultural sector may
indeed mean that a specialized agricultural bank is
more necessary than in Eastern Europe. But as more and
more fixed investment expenditures come to be financed
by means of loans rather than grants, the institutional
bifurcation between the PBC and PCBC (under the supervision of the MOF) may cause difficulties in communication and coordination. The fact that the two
organizations compete for jurisdiction over important
credit categories only makes things worse. In this
case the Chinese departure from the general trend in
Eastern Europe may well be harmful.

FOREIGN DEBT

    There appears to be an inherent tendency for
centrally planned economic systems to accumulate
foreign debt if they are opened up to international
trade with non-Communist countries. The reasons for
this have been enumerated elsewhere and need not be
repeated here.[20] The same tendency seems to be
present even in countries like Yugoslavia and Hungary,
which have undergone considerable economic reforms.
The only sure way to avoid increasing foreign indebtedness and serious debt-servicing problems appears to
be tight administrative controls and a willingness to
cut imports, even at some cost in terms of slower
economic growth and reduced transfer of advanced
technology from abroad. These sacrifices are easier
for large countries like China and the USSR, since
they are less dependent on foreign trade in the first
place. For the smaller countries of Eastern Europe
the costs of restricting imports may be unacceptable,
particularly if misguided policies in the past have

made a country's production process overly
import intensive, as happened in Poland.[21]
China learned of the problems associated with
foreign indebtedness from its experience with the
Soviet Union in the 1950s and early 1960s. Its
perennial caution in this area is based on political
and ideological considerations as well as economic
factors. It could be argued that China has used less
than the optimal amount of foreign debt in financing
its economic development. But given the negative
examples of such countries as Poland and even
Yugoslavia, prudence in this area seems warranted.

A more specific lesson from Eastern Europe in the
sphere of foreign financing of investment is that joint
ventures, compensation trade, processing and assembly,
countertrade, and other foreign exchange saving devices
are likely to have disappointing results. They generate exports but may do so less efficiently than
straightforward methods of export promotion. More
important, the benefits from technology transfer may
have been overrated. Foreign firms in many cases are
willing to share only relatively simple techniques
using out-of-date equipment which may be overpriced.
On the other hand, there are at least two reasons
why the picture in China may not be quite as gloomy as
in Eastern Europe: (1) the greater relative backward-
ness of China means that transfer of a given level of
technology will be more beneficial than in Eastern
Europe; (2) specific complementarities and differential factor endowments in the case of deals with
Hong Kong may make them more rewarding.

GENERAL CONSIDERATIONS

Though they go well beyond the financial system,
two other aspects of Eastern European economic reforms
should receive some mention - price reform and the
problem of exit. For financial indicators to guide
the actions of economic units correctly, prices must
mean something in terms of scarcity values, and more
important they must be responsive to changes in demand
and supply conditions. The effectiveness of economic
reforms in Hungary has been marred by failure to fully
transform the system of price formation. A major
reform started in 1980 is attempting to base prices of
most goods on world prices, with provision for con-
tinuous adjustments.[22] China as a large country need
not be as concerned with matching world relative
prices, but price reform is just as important as it is
in Eastern Europe from the point of view of domestic
economic activities.

A major hindrance to economic reforms in any socialist economy is the fact that bankruptcy of a firm in the state-owned sector is practically unheard of. The threat of exit is almost entirely vacuous. This means that no matter how carefully rewards are calibrated with actual performance, major enterprises know that whatever their actions they will not be allowed to go out of existence. Some authors describe this as a problem of property rights. This characterization is misleading, however. Just because the state owns a factory there is no reason why it can't be dissolved and its physical assets converted to more profitable uses. The impossibility of bankruptcy is more an indication of the claims enterprises have on the state than a result of state ownership. In any case bank credit is unlikely to be an effective sanction unless there is some threat of bankruptcy.

In China at present the threat of shutdown or only slightly more palatable alternatives is more realistic than in other socialist countries, at least for certain classes of enterprises. It is reasonable to suppose that nearly all plants actually being closed down during the current readjustment period are relatively small. Even so, the fact that the very existence of financially troubled firms may be called into question must make bank sanctions as well as more general economic reforms more effective. This presents China with a unique, possibly temporary opportunity to improve enterprise financial management.

Finally, even a superficial look at economic reform in Eastern Europe provides convincing evidence on the following two points: (1) reforms take a great deal of time and generally require considerable modifications during a long process of experimentation, and (2) reforms must be thought out in advance, carefully planned, and well coordinated in order to be successful. In this light the lack of overall coordination of China's economic reforms in general and those involving the banking system in particular becomes all the more glaring.

8
Conclusions

Based on the background information presented in Chapters 2 and 3, the discussion of financial reforms in Chapters 4-6, and the brief review of Eastern European experience in Chapter 7, it is possible to draw some general conclusions. This chapter will make no attempt to summarize the findings of earlier chapters. Instead there will be a brief discussion of the most important financial reforms implemented in China during the past several years. This will be followed by a consideration of the underlying common trends and patterns. Finally, we will look at the future prospects for financial reforms in China and speculate on the likely direction that reforms will take.

INSTITUTIONAL CHANGES

Institutional reforms in China's financial system have focussed on strengthening the independence of the banking system, more clearly separating its role and functions from those of the fiscal system, and restoring and establishing various specialized financial institutions. The most marked feature has been institutional proliferation. The number of organizationally distinct banks and other financial institutions has increased greatly since 1978. In part this is justified by the wider range of activities banks are now engaged in and the greater importance of financial resources and institutions in guiding economic activity. However, much of the institutional proliferation has resulted in overlapping jurisdictions, competition among various institutions, and greater difficulties in coordinating policies. These problems are not new, but they have been exacerbated by the sharp increase in

the number of institutions involved with banking and
finance.

Institutional proliferation beyond a certain
point has probably worked against the objective of
more clearly separating banking and fiscal functions.
Nevertheless the situation is now far better than it
was before 1976, when the PBC was incorporated in the
MOF. At the central level the banking system is now
more independent from the fiscal system. Moreover,
the most obvious form of utilizing the banking system
to solve essentially fiscal problems, deficit financing by means of money creation, is no longer being
practised. Use of the banking system for fiscal
purposes continues in various disguised forms,
however.

On the other side of the coin, some of the new
innovations in banking policy have a strongly fiscal
character. The most prominent example is the mode of
repayment for short- and medium-term equipment loans.
These are supposed to be repaid with incremental
profits from the project financed by the loan, but if
this source is insufficient, depreciation funds and
even various kinds of taxes can be diverted to loan
repayment.[1] Given the relatively short maturities of
these loans, use of taxes and depreciation funds for
repayment may be a common phenomenon. Though probably
designed to make loans attractive to enterprises (they
are virtually risk-free from the latter's perspective)
the mode of repayment means that the granting of these
loans has a potentially profound fiscal impact.

Reforms have unquestionably strengthened the
authority of the banking system at the national level,
and banks have greater freedom to pursue independent
policies. At the local level, however, bank branches
in practice still may not be independent from local
government authorities and finance bureaus. In particular, some bank branches may still be forced to
continue providing credit to inefficient enterprises
that should be closed down. Internal decentralization
of the banking system (discussed below) may have
weakened central control over money and credit without
doing much to ensure that local banks act independently from parochial local government interests.

All in all, the positive achievements of institutional reforms have been in part offset by the adverse
side effects of institutional proliferation, and questions remain about the true degree of independence of
the banking system at the local level. Clear separa-
tion of fiscal and banking institutions, functions,
and jurisdictions is a laudable goal, but it can be
argued that the institutional specialization pursued
in China during the past several years has hindered
rather than furthered this objective.

CHANGES IN THE STRUCTURE OF INTEREST RATES

This is an area in which reforms have been highly successful. Interest rates on individuals' savings deposits have been sharply increased (see Table 10); combined with other policies, interest rate changes have helped make savings much more attractive to the population. The general increase in interest rates on loans to enterprises instituted in 1982 (Table 11) was an important step in rationalizing the structure of interest rates. It probably has provided enterprises with greater incentives to economize on their circulating capital loans; just as important, the increase made banking activities at the margin profitable. Local bank branches have been given some flexibility in setting interest rates.

The main remaining problem is the low interest rates on enterprise deposits and the limited menu of financial assets firms can buy. Even here the introduction of time deposits for organizations in 1982 represents a considerable improvement. The interest paid on enterprise time deposits, however, is probably insufficient to encourage enterprises to invest in these rather than undertaking self-financed investment projects.[2]

What is needed is a long-term financial asset that enterprises can voluntarily buy, which provides them returns sufficient to discourage them from making unwise self-financed investments. Provisions would have to be made for enterprise retention and discretionary use of the interest income earned. Though without more careful study it is impossible to determine what interest rate would be appropriate, a rough guess is that an annual rate of 8 percent might be necessary. Unless loan rates are also raised, this might necessitate a budget subsidy or the explicit use of these assets as a budget deficit financing device. This would entail raising the interest rate on Treasury bonds to the point where enterprises purchase large amounts of them voluntarily. To function effectively as an alternative to self-financed investment, the sales of these financial assets should not be geared toward the needs of deficit financing but rather toward providing appropriate incentives for enterprises.

INTERNAL DECENTRALIZATION OF THE BANKING SYSTEM

Internal decentralization and reform of the banking system has involved: (1) transforming banks into profit-oriented business enterprises whose

employees are eligible to earn bonuses; (2) allowing
lower-level bank branches to make some reallocations
among different categories of loans, as long as they
meet aggregate targets; and (3) letting banks that
attract more deposits than planned or speed up the
turnover of their loans use the proceeds to make
additional loans of their choice. The goal is the
obvious one of improving the allocation of bank credit
and the efficiency and flexibility of bank operations.

Decentralization has been successful in substantially increasing the incentives for lower-level bank
branches to attract deposits and economize on planned
loans. We have already seen, however, that this new
system is potentially inflationary.[3] Recently, it has
been criticized not on the grounds that it is inflationary but rather because it removes larger and
larger amounts of loan funds from the control of
higher-level banks (mainly provincial branches).[4]
This is said to hinder attempts to centralize financial resources and exacerbates the problem of dupli-
cative, inefficient local investment. If this
judgment is correct, it implies that mobility of funds
within the banking system has decreased as a result of
decentralization. Bank branches apparently are
holding on to their deposits in order to turn around
and grant more loans, rather than willingly depositing
their excess funds with higher-level bank branches for
reallocation through the banking system. This problem
might be ameliorated by higher interest rates on
interbranch deposits.

The decentralized credit management system may
also have contributed to the difficulties China faces
in controlling the aggregate level and composition of
investment. Even if the new system applies only to
circulating capital loans, it may well have hindered
attempts to improve the efficiency of working capital
investment. But neither of these effects may be significant when compared with the impact of other trends
and policy changes (such as fiscal decentralization
and loan financing of fixed investment).

FISCAL DECENTRALIZATION

Fiscal decentralization has been more radical and
more significant in its impact than decentralization
of the banking system. Provincial governments now
share in the revenues generated in their territories;
they can keep a large proportion of revenues above
their actual revenue in 1979. This system is supposed
to remain unchanged through 1985. Its impact has been
diluted, however, by the involuntary loans exacted by

the central government from provinces starting in 1981
as well as to a lesser extent sales of Treasury bonds.
Nevertheless, fiscal decentralization almost certainly
has increased the discretionary financial resources
available to provincial governments. Since provincial
and local authorities have been eager to expand
investment activities in the areas under their jurisdiction, this has exacerbated the central government's
difficulties in controlling the aggregate level of
investment. This in turn has hindered improvements in
the efficiency of investment.

The impact of fiscal decentralization thus on the
whole appears to have been negative. The measures
appear not to have resulted in any extraordinary
increases in revenue. Total budgetary revenues of all
levels of government have not risen rapidly in the
years since the decentralization measures were introduced (see Table 6). It is possible that decentralization prevented deterioration in the revenue situation,
and that local governments now use funds more efficiently than they did in the past. These possible
beneficial effects are hard to gauge but are almost
certainly more than offset by the adverse impact of
fiscal decentralization on the structure and
efficiency of investment.

A recent article in the Chinese press has criticized the fiscal decentralization measures on three
grounds: (1) Though revenues were decentralized, the
burden of financial expenditures on the central
government remains great; hence makeshift measures
like involuntary loans from the localities and
Treasury bond issues became necessary. (2) Combined
with the distorted structure of relative prices, the
decentralization has resulted in blind, excessive
production of high-priced commodities in many areas.
(3) The fact that quotas and sharing rates are fixed
for years in advance hinders readjustment policies.[5]
The article does not recommend that fiscal decentralization be rescinded, but it recognizes that this is
not a fruitful direction for future reforms. A State
Council circular issued at the end of 1982 addresses
some of the problems later cited in the press article.
With the exception of Guangdong and Fujian, all
provinces and autonomous regions are to share in a
fixed proportion of their total revenues. Moreover,
provincial expenditure quotas are to be adjusted
downward to obviate the necessity for involuntary
loans from the provinces to the central government.[6]

LOAN FINANCING OF FIXED INVESTMENT

Credit financing of fixed investment has become quite widespread in China during the past several years. Two main channels have been used: (1) substitution of PCBC capital construction loans for budgetary capital construction appropriations and (2) rapidly expanding noncapital construction loans for fixed investment provided by the PBC and other specialized banks. Credit financing reportedly has resulted in greater efficiency in the use of investment funds, and some loan-financed projects have had extremely high returns.

However, any improvements in micro-level efficiency have not led to major improvements in the efficiency of aggregate fixed investment. The main cause of poor returns on aggregate investment in China has been sectoral misallocations rather than deteriorating efficiency in construction operations (though that also has been a factor). Credit financing can lead to improvements in the latter, but in the absence of other measures probably does not do much to ameliorate problems with the sectoral allocation of investment. Indeed, in an environment with a highly distorted price system, profit-oriented investment decisions may cause a deterioration in the overall economic efficiency of investment. Finally, if it makes more financial resources for investment available to enterprises (unquestionably this has occurred in China), credit financing exacerbates the problem of excessive demand for investment goods.

FINANCIAL INTERMEDIATION

The Chinese banking system has made some tentative moves toward becoming a true financial intermediary channeling financial resources from surplus to deficit units. The most important measures have been the decentralization of the credit management system and the establishment of domestic trust and investment organizations. The potential and actual problems of the decentralization of credit management have already been discussed. The financial intermediation involved in trust work has also been subjected to criticism in the Chinese press. In addition to the prohibition on trust organizations not sponsored by banks in early 1982, suggestions have been made that trust activities established by banks should be subjected to tighter supervision.[7] More recently it has been required that investments financed by trust organizations should be included in the comprehensive state investment plan and in the state credit plan.[8]

In an environment where investment demand chronically exceeds the supply of investment goods by a wide margin and central authorities have experienced great difficulties in reducing the aggregate level of investment, the harmful effects of the financial intermediation activities China has experimented with during the past few years may well outweigh any positive results. This is particularly true of trust work, whose main effect may be to concentrate small, scattered bits of excess demand and transform them into significant excess demand in the investment sector.

MAIN PATTERNS

Are there any common threads that tie together the specific problems encountered by the various concrete financial reform measures? One is the focus on micro-level efficiency improvements and neglect of macroeconomic problems. By and large reforms have not been designed specifically to solve macroeconomic difficulties or at least ensure that foreseeable macroeconomic side effects can be dealt with as an integral part of the reform package. Instead, emerging macroeconomic problems have been attacked by ad-hoc administrative measures as they come up. This tendency may have harmed some of the incentives that are supposed to be fostered by reforms; an example of this is the involuntary loans and Treasury bond sales used to ameliorate imbalances caused by fiscal decentralization. More important, neglect of macroeconomic aspects renders broadening and expanding reforms more difficult.

Many financial reforms have exacerbated difficulties in controlling aggregate investment demand. Reforms have provided greater access to discretionary financial resources for enterprises and local governments, which have used the extra funds for investment. In this situation the central government is faced with difficult choices if it wants to restrict aggregate investment: (1) rescind reforms or essentially negate their impact through ad-hoc administrative measures; (2) cut investment in priority sectors like energy and transport, where there are many large projects financed by budget allocations; or (3) let investment be reduced by bottlenecks in the supply of investment goods, with consequent hoarding, excessive project starts, competition for supplies, etc. None of these alternatives is attractive, yet in some cases cancellation of certain financial reforms may well be called for as the least damaging course of action, at least in the short run.

Another common pattern is the pervasiveness of
institutional aspects and constraints. With many new
specialized institutional actors on the scene, it has
become more difficult to coordinate policies. Jurisdictional disputes sometimes hinder the financial
system's attempts to implement the most appropriate
reforms. Competition among institutions may be one
factor causing banks to provide investment financing
too easily.

Many of the reforms considered in this study have
involved decentralization of authority and financial
resources. Despite undoubted benefits in many cases,
decentralization in the absence of certain complementary measures may prove to be more harmful than
beneficial. This is particularly true for the banking
system, which is envisaged as guiding economic
activity (by indirect means) after full-scale reforms
have been implemented. Thus it is not necessarily
true that decentralization in the banking sphere or in
state finance should proceed as far as it does in the
case of industry or commerce.

PROGNOSIS

Aside from the four common patterns mentioned in
the preceding section, a marked characteristic of
reforms in China's financial system has been the lack
of a consistent overall vision of the role of the
banking system in a reformed socialist economy. There
are at least four views of the role of the banking
system underlying Chinese policies.

In the first perspective, banks are seen as
supporters of production whose main task is to ensure
that shortages of funds never become a bottleneck
hampering enterprise operations on the micro level or
the growth of output on the macro level. The idea
that banks should freely supply funds for production
goes back at least as far as 1958 and was a dominant
theme of the "Gang of Four" period.

The view of banks as representatives of the state
that supervise enterprise financial activities to
verify that plans are fulfilled and sound financial
management practised was inherited by China as an
integral part of the Soviet model. The use of the
banking system to implement administrative restrictions in support of readjustment policies is an
extension of this role.

The current conventional wisdom in China that
banks should use indirect "economic levers" rather
than administrative directives in supervising their
clients is related to the conception in the Soviet

model. The shift from direct to indirect control
mechanisms is such a drastic one, however, that this
viewpoint should be clearly differentiated from the
second perspective.

Finally, in the past two or three years suggestions for reform as well as some concrete policy
measures have been based on the belief that bank
branches should be independent, profit-oriented
business firms using negotiations and economic contracts to deal with enterprises. This would require
establishing a central bank to carry out state policy
(using indirect macroeconomic devices rather than
direct supervision of individual firms), in addition
to an industrial and commercial banking network to
handle credit and other banking services for enterprises. Actions taken so far have given bank branches
more independence while not making major institutional
changes. More important, no indirect tools with which
the central bank can affect the aggregate level of
economic activity have been devised.

Conflicts between the first and the other three
conceptions have received some attention in Chinese
scholarly articles, but it is generally believed that
they can coexist as long as the first does not domin-
ate. There is little recognition, however, that a
banking system of profit-oriented business firms (the
fourth possible role) can subvert attempts to use the
banking system as an instrument of macroeconomic
control (the second and third roles). China apparently has not yet determined what role the banking
system should play in a reformed economy. This makes
promulgation and implementation of consistent policies
difficult and hinders their effectiveness, since some
measures may work at cross-purposes.

We have already seen that contradictions between
specific banking policies and the overall economic
goals of the authorities have proved to be a significant problem. Certain banking reforms may exacerbate
inflationary pressures. Others provide means for
firms to get around cutbacks in state-budgeted investment appropriations by seeking various kinds of loans.
Trust and investment corporations have at least the
potential of removing significant transactions and
investment decisions from the direct supervision of
banks. The list could go on. The Chinese approach to
these contradictions so far has emphasized nullifying
the harmful side effects of reforms by means of
administrative measures rather than rescinding the
reforms themselves. It is likely that further progress in financial reforms will be limited unless the
pattern of micro-oriented reforms leading to macroeconomic problems leading to ad-hoc administrative

restrictions is broken. More specifically, innovations like the establishment of a separate central
bank are likely to have only limited benefits until
effective indirect macroeconomic policy instruments
are devised, particularly nonadministrative control
mechanisms within the banking system.

Another area where continuing problems are likely
to hinder reform efforts and obstruct improvements in
efficiency is investment financing. Difficulties are
likely to continue for the foreseeable future.
Attempts by the central authorities to recentralize
control over investment decisionmaking will run up
against existing financial reforms. We may well see
some at least temporary retreats on reforms like the
decentralized credit management system and even loan
financing of fixed investment. Following the pattern
of the past several years, these are more likely to
involve strengthened administrative controls rather
than outright cancellation of major reform measures,
but the latter cannot be ruled out in the case of the
most controversial reforms.

The role of the banking system as an active
financial intermediary has already come under some
criticism and probably will remain problematic in the
future. Thus we can expect that trust activities
will be subjected to even tighter control in the future
and probably will be significantly cut back. Tighter
control may be exercised over credit planning and
management as well.

This chapter has paid more attention to the
problems encountered by China's financial reforms than
to their positive achievements. Since future reform
policies will be responses to these problems, this
focus is appropriate. But it must be recognized that
significant benefits have already been realized by the
reforms, and that reform policies will continue to be
broadened and strengthened in certain areas. Most of
the problems encountered have not been the result of
inherent flaws in the reform measures themselves. For
the most part difficulties have been caused by
problems of coordination, inappropriate timing in the
introduction of some of the reforms, and the absence
of certain key complementary reforms. Therefore, if
improvements can be made in these areas the future
prognosis for financial sector reforms in China is
bright.

Tables

TABLE 1
China's State Banking Statistics /a
(in million yuan)

SOURCES OF FUNDS	End 1979	End 1980	% increase over 1979	End 1981	% increase over 1980	End 1982	% increase over 1981
Deposits							
Deposits by enterprises	134,004	165,864	23.8	200,558	20.9	228,714	14.0
Deposits by the treasury	46,891	57,309	22.2	67,407	17.6	71,788	6.5
Capital construction funds	14,868	16,202	9.0	19,494	20.3	17,576	-9.8
	13,130	17,175	30.8	22,915	33.4	28,480	24.3
Deposits by government departments and organizations	18,488	22,945	24.1	27,488	19.8	33,143	20.6
Savings deposits in cities and towns	20,256	28,249	39.5	35,414	25.4	44,733	26.3
Deposits in rural areas /b	20,371	23,843	1.7	27,840	16.1	32,994	18.5
Deposits by international monetary institutions	-	3,427		5,405	57.7	5,241	-3.0
Currency in circulation	26,771	34,620	29.3	39,634	14.5	43,912	10.8
The bank's working funds /c	42,788	47,733	11.6	49,705	-4.1	51,829	4.3
The bank's surplus	4,945	1,972	-45.0	1,722	-12.7	3,668	113.0
Others	7,752	8,810	4.0	7,762	11.9	8,160	5.1
Total Credit Funds	216,260	262,426	21.4	304,786	16.1	341,524	12.1

TABLE 1 (Cont'd)
China's State Banking Statistics /a
(in million yuan)

USES OF FUNDS	End 1979	End 1980	% increase over 1979	End 1981	% increase over 1980	End 1982	% increase over 1981
Loans							
To industrial production enterprises /d	203,963	241,430	18.4	276,467	14.5	305,227	10.4
To industrial supply and marketing enterprises and materials supply departments /d	36,309	43,158	18.9	50,885	17.9	52,672	3.5
Commercial loans /a	24,212	23,603	-2.5	24,124	2.2	23,985	-0.6
Short- and medium-term loans for buying equipment	123,225	143,702	16.6	163,913	14.1	178,821	9.1
Industrial and commercial loans to urban collective and individual enterprises /a	792	5,550	600.86	8,375	50.9	15,198	81.5
For earnest money	5,751	7,829	36.1	9,915	26.6	13,306	34.2
To state farms	698	788	12.9	739	-6.2	743	0.5
To rural communes and production brigades	686	940	37.0	1,675	78.2	1,981	18.3
Gold purchases	12,290	15,860	29.0	16,841	6.2	18,521	10.0
Foreign exchange purchases	1,216	1,216		1,204	-1.0	1,204	0
Balances with the IMF	2,058	-847		6,218	-	14,279	129.6
	-	3,604		3,874	7.5	3,791	-2.1
Money advanced to the Ministry of Finance /e	9,023	17,023	88.7	17,023	0	17,023	0
Total Credit Funds Used	216,260	262,426	21.4	304,786	16.1	341,524	12.1

TABLE 1 (Cont'd)
China's State Banking Statistics /a
(in million yuan)

/a   Consolidated accounts of the PBC, ABC (but not the rural credit coopera-
    tives, for which figures are given in Table 3) and BOC (domestic currency
    accounts only).

/b   Presumably includes deposits by rural credit cooperatives in the ABC as well
    as other deposits in the latter.

/c   Includes allocations for bank credit funds in the state budget and the accu-
    mulated profits which the bank is allowed to keep (BJR, No. 29, 7/20/81,
    p. 23).

/d   Loans of circulating funds (working capital).

/e   An accumulated budget surplus was run down in 1979; the actual budget defi-
    cit in that year was 17.06 billion yuan (Wang Bingqian (1980), p. 51).

Source: BJR No. 29, 7/20/81, p. 21; ZGJR, No. 4, 4/4/83, p. 61.
       State Statistical Bureau (1982), p. 399.

TABLE 2:
Long-Term Growth Rates of Various Financial
Aggregates /a

Items	Average annual growth rate (% per year)
Currency in Circulation /b	
1953-57	7.5
1957-62	15.1
1962-65	-5.2
1965-70	6.3
1970-75	8.1
1975-78	5.1
1978-81	23.2
1957-81	8.8
Individual Deposits	
1953-57	32.6
1957-62	3.1
1962-65	16.6
1965-70	4.0
1970-75	13.5
1975-78	12.1
1978-81	35.5
1957-81	11.9
Enterprise Deposits /c	
1957-62	30.9
1962-65	6.1
1965-70	4.4
1970-75	9.9
1975-78	0.5
1978-81	22.3
1957-81	12.5
Money Supply /d	
1957-62	18.6
1962-65	4.0
1965-70	4.4
1970-75	10.6
1975-78	4.4
1978-81	26.3
1957-81	11.1

TABLE 2 (Cont'd)
Long-Term Growth Rates of Various Financial
Aggregates /a

Items	Average annual growth rate (% per year)
Loans to Enterprises /e	
1957–62	19.8
1962–65	–2.6
1965–70	10.7
1970–75	8.0
1975–78	7.7
1978–80	13.4
1957–80	10.0

/a Compound growth rates from year end to year end.

/b Based on the following index number series for currency in circulation at the end of the year:

1953	75	1962	202	1971	258
1954	78	1963	170	1972	286
1955	76	1964	152	1973	315
1956	108	1965	172	1974	334
1957	100	1966	205	1975	346
1958	128	1967	231	1976	386
1959	142	1968	254	1977	370
1960	182	1969	260	1978	402
1961	238	1970	234	1979	507

To obtain actual amounts for earlier years, the ratio of the index numbers for each earlier year to that for 1977 was multiplied by the value of currency outstanding at the end of 1977. For 1978–81, actual figures were used.

/c This is the same as the "deposits by enterprises" item in Table 1. Figures for earlier years were obtained from the following index number series for enterprise deposits:

1957	100.0	1970	569.5	1978	928.0
1962	383.6	1975	913.6	1979	1,181.1
1965	458.2	1977	969.0	1980	1,413.1

As in the case of currency in circulation, 1977 was used as the base year in determining amounts, and actual statistics were used for 1978–81.

139

TABLE 2 (Cont'd)
Long-Term Growth Rates of Various Financial
Aggregates /a

/d Sum of the preceding three items. It is incomplete because
it does not include enterprise deposits at the PCBC or
deposits of rural collectives and commune and brigade enterprises at the rural credit cooperatives. On the other hand,
a large proportion of individual deposits consists of time
deposits, and there are restrictions on the use of most
enterprise deposits.

/e Based on an index number series whose exact scope is not
clear. Most likely it includes all loans to urban state-
owned enterprises.

1957	100.0	1970	379.6	1979	761.7
1962	246.4	1975	556.5	1980	892.1
1965	227.9	1978	694.3		

Source: Tables 1 and 12; ZGBKNJ (1981), p. 207; BJR, No. 29,
7/20/81, p.21; Yu Guantao (1981) p. 47; ZGJR, No. 5,
3/4/82, p. 49; International Financial Statistics,
November 1982, pp. 120-121.

TABLE 3
Deposits and Loans of Rural Credit Cooperatives (in million yuan)

Items	End 1979	End 1980	% increase over 1979	End 1981	% increase over 1980	End 1982	% increase over 1981
Total deposits	21,588	27,234	26.2	31,961	17.4	38,988	22.0
Deposits by communes and brigades	9,833	10,548	7.3	11,324	7.4	12,106	6.9
Deposits by commune- and brigade-run enterprises	2,193	2,947	34.4	2,973	0.9	3,366	13.2
Deposits by commune members	7,843	11,703	49.2	16,955	44.9	22,811	34.5
Others	1,719	2,035	18.4	709	-65.2	705	-0.6
Total loans	4,754	8,164	71.7	9,638	18.1	12,115	25.7
Agricultural loans to communes and brigades	2,254	3,454	53.2	3,571	3.4	3,476	-2.7
Loans to commune- and brigade-run enterprises	1,415	3,111	119.9	3,546	14.0	4,230	19.3
Loans to individual commune members	1,085	1,599	47.4	2,521	57.7	4,409	74.9

Source: BJR, No. 29, 7/20/81, pp. 21-22; State Statistical Bureau (1982), p. 400; ZGJR, No. 4, 4/4/83, p. 61.

TABLE 4

Bank of China Balance Sheet (Current US$ million as of December 31, 1977-79) /a

	1977	% change	1978	% change	1979	% change	1979 sub-totals as % of total
Assets							
Cash	26.4	19.0	31.8	20.1	39.6	24.8	0.1
Due from banks	6,260.1	14.9	7,547.2	20.6	11,659.8	54.5	33.3
Bills discounted and remittances bought	1,192.2	18.0	1,747.8	46.6	2,374.9	35.9	6.8
Loans and overdrafts	2,965.6	-0.3	4,254.1	43.5	7,035.1	65.4	20.1
Securities and investments	41.8	27.4	56.6	35.5	74.9	32.3	0.2
Land, buildings, furniture, and equipment	95.4	49.3	141.2	48.0	212.5	50.5	0.6
Sundry accounts receivable, including those under forward contracts	474.2	20.1	608.9	28.4	823.1	35.2	2.4
Collections receivable for customers	230.7	6.4	338.2	68.3	679.7	75.1	1.9
Customers' liabilities under letters of credit guarantee	4,582.8	15.9	7,533.5	64.4	11,273.2	49.6	32.2
Trust assets	153.8	-24.9	175.5	14.1	200.6	14.3	0.6
Other assets	440.5	784.6	527.8	19.8	631.6	19.7	1.8
Total Assets	16,463.4	14.6	23,012.7	39.8	35,005.0	52.1	100.0
Profit and Loss Statement							
General expenses	81.9	33.8	127.5	55.6	389.8	205.8	61.0
Depreciation and amortization	49.7	30.5	69.4	39.6	99.8	43.8	15.6
Net profit	67.6	26.7	97.9	44.7	149.0	52.2	23.4
Total Expenses	199.3	30.5	294.8	47.9	638.6	116.6	100.0

TABLE 4 (Cont'd)
Bank of China Balance Sheet (Current US$ million as of December 31, 1977-79) /a

	1977	% change	1978	% change	1979	% change	1979 sub-totals as % of total
Total Interest, Commissions and Other Income	199.3	30.5	294.8	47.9	638.6	116.6	100.0
Liabilities							
Due to banks	3,588.1	-1.8	4,182.4	16.6	7,068.0	69.0	20.2
Deposits	6,868.9	25.9	9,375.5	36.5	13,906.1	48.3	39.7
Remittances and drafts outstanding	61.9	17.2	101.7	56.6	185.3	82.2	0.5
Sundry accounts payable, including those under forward contracts	363.3	17.9	471.7	29.8	644.8	36.7	1.9
Collections for customers	230.7	6.4	388.2	68.3	679.7	75.1	1.9
Letters of credit and guarantee	4,582.8	15.9	7,533.5	64.4	11,273.2	49.6	32.2
Trust liabilities	153.8	-24.9	175.5	14.1	200.6	14.3	0.6
Other liabilities	84.6	13.3	115.7	36.7	152.1	31.5	0.4
Total Liabilities	15,937.1	14.5	22,344.2	40.2	34,109.8	52.7	97.4

TABLE 4 (Cont'd)
Bank of China Balance Sheet (Current US$ million as of December 31, 1977-79) /a

	1977	% change	1978	% change	1979	% change	1979 sub-totals as % of total
Net Worth							
Capital	215.8	4.4	237.8	10.2	258.2	8.6	0.7
Surplus	103.5	36.8	148.8	43.8	199.4	33.9	0.6
Reserves	139.5	24.5	184.0	31.8	288.6	56.9	0.8
Net profit current year	67.6	26.7	97.9	44.7	149.0	52.2	0.5
Total Net Worth	526.4	17.6	668.5	27.0	895.2	33.9	2.6
Total Liabilities and Net Worth	16,463.4	14.6	23,012.7	39.8	35,005.0	52.1	100.0

/a Conversion factors based on period average yuan-dollar exchange rates of 1.854 in 1977, 1.682 in 1978 and 1.549 in 1979. Percentage increases are based on unrounded 1976-79 balance sheet figures.

Source: CBR, July-August 1980, pp. 12, 13.

TABLE 5
The People's Insurance Company of China 1979 International Accounts

	Yuan million	US$ million [a]
Profit and Loss Statement		
Income		
Premiums – Direct insurance [b]	171.2	110.5
– Inward insurance [c]	204.0	131.7
– Less: reinsurance ceded	72.3	46.7
Reserve fund, at beginning of year	94.8	61.2
Investment, interest and other income	33.7	21.8
Total	431.4	278.5
Outflow		
Claims – Direct business	88.0	56.8
– Inward reinsurance	139.0	89.7
– Less: reinsurance ceded	41.0	26.5
Commissions – Direct business	26.6	17.1
– Inward reinsurance	57.4	37.1
– Less: reinsurance ceded	21.9	14.2
General expenses and other expenditures	18.1	11.7
Balance of profit and loss statement	44.0	28.4
Reserve fund, at end of year	121.2	78.2
Total	431.4	278.5

TABLE 5 (Cont'd)
The People's Insurance Company of China 1979 International Accounts

	Yuan million	US$ million /a
Balance Sheet		
Assets		
Fixed assets	5.7	3.7
Cash and bond deposits	554.3	357.8
Investments	27.7	17.9
Premiums receivable	16.4	10.6
Due from companies and other entities	26.4	17.0
Deposits held by reinsurers	67.4	43.5
Sundry debtors	7.2	4.7
Total	705.1	455.2
Liabilities		
Government capital	50.0	32.3
Statutory reserve	85.3	55.1
General reserve	250.0	161.4
Insurance fund	121.2	78.2
Claims reserve	90.3	58.3
Other reserve	12.8	8.2
Due to companies and other entities	13.6	8.8
Deposits held for reinsurers	32.1	20.7
Sundry creditors	5.4	3.5
Overall profit /d - Brought forward	0.4	0.3
- Current year	44.0	28.4
Total	705.1	455.2

146

TABLE 5 (Cont'd)
The People's Insurance Company of China 1979 International Accounts

/a Dollar amounts based on unrounded RMB figures using exchange rate of
    Y 1.549 per $1.
/b 24.84% more than the 1978 figure of Y 137.1 million ($88.5 million).
/c 27.92% more than the 1978 figure of Y 159.5 million ($103.0 million).
/d 11.79% more than the 1978 profit of Y 39.8 million ($25.7 million).

Source: CBR, March-April 1981, p.39.

TABLE 6
State Budget Revenues (in million yuan) /a

	1977	1978/b	1979	1980	1981	1982 (estimate)	1983 (forecast)
Total Revenue	87,450	112,110	110,330	108,523	108,946	110,690	123,200
Enterprise profit remittances /c	n.a.	57,200	49,290	43,524	35,368	31,100	32,390
Of which: Industrial enterprise profit remittances	32,814	44,100	n.a.	44,920	/d	n.a.	n.a.
Taxes	n.a.	51,900	53,780	57,170	62,989	67,950	72,970
Of which: Industrial-commercial tax	40,090	45,200	n.a.	50,135	/d	n.a.	n.a.
Agricultural tax	n.a.	2,800	n.a.	2,767	/d	n.a.	n.a.
Treasury bonds /e	-	-	-	-	/f	n.a.	n.a.
Foreign loans	n.a./g	200	3,530	4,301	7,308	7,440	5,400
Other /h	n.a.	2,800	3,730	3,528	3,281	7,440	8,440/i

TABLE 6 (Cont'd)
State Budget Revenues (in million yuan) /a

/a Consolidated budgetary accounts of all levels of government.

/b Individual components are based on percentage breakdowns in State Statistical Bureau (1982), p. 396, and are rounded off to the nearest Y 100 million.

/c These come entirely from state-owned units. Starting in 1980 the profit remittances of state-owned industrial enterprises are larger than the total for all state-owned units, meaning that nonindustrial state enterprises were subsidized on a net basis.

/d Preliminary figures for these items in 1981 were: industrial enterprise profit remittances Y 41,114 million, industrial-commercial tax receipts Y 53,905 million, and agricultural tax receipts Y 2,811 million.

/e No Treasury bonds were issued before 1981.

/f A total of Y 4,866 million worth of Treasury bonds were sold in 1981, but this amount was not formally included in the accounts of any year as budgetary revenue.

/g Foreign loans in 1977 most likely were very small.

/h Derived as a residual. Includes depreciation funds handed over to central authorities averaging somewhat more than Y2 billion each year in 1978-1983.

/i Including a new category of revenue called "construction funds for key projects in energy and transport."

Source: State Budget Reports in BJR, No. 29, 7/20/79, pp. 17-24, No. 39, 9/29/80, pp. 11-23, and No. 2, 1/11/82, pp. 14-23; additional State Budget Reports dated 8/23/82 and 12/10/82 (translated in BBC FE7117, 8/30/82, pp. C2-C6 and FE7209, 12/15/82, pp. C2/1-C2/10, respectively; State Statistical Bureau (1982), pp. 395-397; Xu Yi and Chen Yulin (1982), pp. 12-17.

TABLE 7
State Budget Expenditures (in million yuan) /a

	1977	1978	1979	1980	1981	1982 (estimate)	1983 (forecast)
Total Expenditure	84,350	111,100	127,390	121,273	111,497	113,690	126,200
Capital construction	30,088	45,192	51,470	41,939	33,063	30,270	36,180
Of which: Financed by foreign loans	n.a./b	n.a./b	7,090	7,300	7,308	5,000	5,400
Modernization of existing enterprises and new product development	n.a./c	n.a./c	7,200	8,045	6,530	6,070	6,570
Additional circulating funds for enterprises /d	n.a./c	n.a./c	5,200	3,671	2,284	2,300	2,250
Aid to agriculture	5,068	7,695	9,010	8,210	7,368	7,650	7,750
Education, culture, public health, and science	9,020	11,266	13,210	15,626	17,136	19,000	20,400
Defense	14,910	16,784	22,270	19,384	16,797	17,870	17,870
Administration	4,332	4,908	5,690	6,679	7,088	8,000	8,500
Other /e	n.a.	n.a.	13,340	17,719	21,231	22,530	26,680
Budget Surplus /f	3,100	1,010	-17,060	-12,750	-2,551	-3,000	-3,000

TABLE 7 (Cont'd)
State Budget Expenditures (in million yuan) /a

/a Consolidated budgetary accounts of all levels of government.
/b Only small amounts of state budgeted capital construction investment were financed by foreign loans in 1977 and 1978.
/c Total spending on existing enterprises (not just the two categories given here) was Y 13,680 million in 1977 and Y 16,780 million in 1978.
/d The 1979 figure also includes appropriations of credit funds for banks; later figures apparently do not.
/e Derived as a residual, it includes expenditures like repayments of principal and interest on foreign loans, payment of interest on domestic loans from the PBC, social relief, and employment creation.
/f Deficits are indicated by a minus sign.

Source: State Budget Reports in BJR, No. 29, 7/20/79, pp. 17-24, No. 39, 9/29/80, pp. 11-23, and No. 2, 1/11/82, pp. 14-23; additional State Budget Reports dated 8/23/82 and 12/10/82 (translated in BBC FE/117, 8/30/82, pp. C2-C6 and FE/209, 12/15/82, pp. C2/1-C2/10, respectively); State Statistical Bureau (1982), pp. 395-397; Xu Yi and Chen Yulin (1982), pp. 12-17.

TABLE 8
Average Wages in China's State Sector

Year	Average annual wage (yuan per employee)		
	State sector as a whole	Industry	Banking and insurance
1952	446	515	458
1957	637	690	613
1962	592	652	559
1965	652	729	624
1970	609	661	588
1975	613	644	609
1977	602	632	622
1978	644	683	643
1979	705	758	675
1980	803	854	760
1981	812	852	787
1982	836	n.a.	n.a.

Source: State Statistical Bureau (1982), p. 426. State Statistical Bureau Communique, 4/29/83; translated in BBC FE7323, 5/3/83, p. C11

152

TABLE 9 .
Current Interest Rates on Loans and Deposits of Economic Units

Item	Monthly rate (%)	Annual rate (%)
Demand Deposits		
Enterprises, departments, and organizations	0.15	1.80
Rural credit cooperatives (at the ABC) /a	0.27	3.24
Interbranch deposits /a	0.27	3.24
Time Deposits		
One year fixed term	0.30	3.60
Two year fixed term	0.36	4.32
Three year fixed term	0.42	5.04
Industrial and Commercial Loans /b		
Circulating capital loans (to state enterprises, collective enterprises, and individual businesses)	0.60	7.20
Urban collective enterprises formed by intellectual youth (during their first two years of operations only) /a	0.36	4.32
Account settlement loans	0.60	7.20
Short- and medium-term equipment purchase loans:		
Under one year maturity	0.42	5.04
One to three years maturity	0.48	5.76
Three to five years maturity	0.54	6.48
Capital construction loans /a	-	3.00

TABLE 9 (Cont'd)
Current Interest Rates on Loans and Deposits of Economic Units

Item	Monthly rate (%)	Annual rate (%)
Agricultural and Related Loans		
To state farms, rural communes and brigades, and commune and brigade enterprises for production expenses /c	0.48	5.76
To state farms for equipment purchases /c	0.42	5.04
To rural communes and brigades and commune and brigade enterprises for equipment and purchases /c	0.36	4.32
For advance purchases	0.48	5.76
To grain enterprises /a	0.21	2.52
To rural credit cooperatives (by the ABC) /a	0.18	2.16
To individual commune members	0.48-0.60	5.76-7.20

/a Interest rates on these types of loans and deposits may have been raised as part of the 1982 general readjustment of rates, but specific information is not available.

/b Overdue loans carry a 20% higher interest rate; loans that are misused or diverted to inappropriate uses carry a penalty rate 50% above the standard interest rate.

/c Loans to rural units which are used to finance industrial or commercial activities are supposed to carry the corresponding interest charges for industrial and commercial loans.

Source: PBC, Planning Bureau (1980), p. 20; ZGJR, No. 9, 9/30/80, p. 16; ZGJR, No. 2, 1/19/82, p. 6; ZGJJNJ (1981), p. II-138.

TABLE 10
Monthly Interest Rates on Individuals' Bank Deposits (in %) /a

Type of deposit	Jan 1953	Sep 1954	Oct 1958	Jan 1959	Jun 1959	Jul 1959	Jun 1965	Oct 1971	Apr 1979	Apr 1980	Apr 1982
Demand Deposits (Passbook)	0.45	0.45	0.24	0.18	0.18	0.18	0.18	0.18	0.18	0.24/b	0.24
Time Deposits											
Installment deposit and lump-sum withdrawal /c											
Three-month term	0.80	0.81	0.42	–	0.24	0.24	–	0.27	0.30	0.36	0.39
Six-month term	0.90	0.90	0.51	0.30	0.30	0.39	0.27	–	0.30	0.36	0.36
One-year term	1.20	1.20	0.66	0.40	0.40	0.51	0.33	0.27	0.33	0.45	0.48
Three-year term	–	–	–	–	–	0.542	–	–	0.375	0.51	0.57
Five-year term	–	–	–	–	–	–	–	–	0.42	0.57	0.66
Eight-year term	–	–	–	–	–	–	–	–	–	–	0.75

/a Except where otherwise indicated, when no figure is provided that means no Deposit of that type was available to savers at that particular time.

/b Increase actually took effect in July 1980.

/c No information is available on deposits of this type in earlier years, but it is quite likely that they were in existence. The term is one year.

Source: ZGBKNJ (1981), p. 208; ZGJR, No. 1, 4/30/79, p. 22; ZGJR, No. 4, 4/30/80, p. 18; ZGJR, No. 2, 1/19/82, p. 6.

TABLE 11
Historical Trend of Monthly Interest Rates on Various Types of Loans
(in % per month)

Item	August 1953	October 1955	January 1958	1959	May 1961	Before September 1972	After 1972	Before January 1982	After 1982 (current)
To state industrial enterprises for working capital	0.45 to 0.48	0.48	0.60	0.60	0.60	0.48	0.42	0.42	0.60
To state commercial enterprises for working capital	0.69	0.60	0.60	0.60	0.60	0.60	0.42/a	0.42	0.60
To agricultural collectives and state farms	0.75	0.60	0.48	0.60	0.48	0.48	0.36	0.36	0.48

TABLE 11 (Cont'd)
Historical Trend of Monthly Interest Rates on Various Types of Loans
(in % per month)

Item	August 1953	October 1955	January 1958	1959	May 1961	Before September 1972	After 1972	Before January 1982	After 1982 (current)
To rural credit cooperatives	1.20	0.90	0.51	-	-	-	-	0.18	n.a.
To individual peasants	0.75	0.75	0.72	0.60	0.48	-	-	0.36/b]	0.48-0.72]
- For production	1.00	0.90	0.72	0.60	-	-	-	0.36/b]	0.72]

/a One source states that this change took place in 1971.

/b Refers only to loans by rural credit cooperatives to their members.

Sources: To rural credit cooperatives and individual peasants for production in 1953-59, Hsiao (1971), Table V-5, p.131. All others 1953-61, Chen, Nai-ruenn (1967), Table 10.32, p.470. Before and after September 1972, Cassou (1973), p.91. Before and after January 1982 from ZGJR, No. 2, 1/19/82, p. 6.

TABLE 12
Individual Savings Deposits in China (in million yuan)/a

| Year | Total savings deposits | Urban savings deposits | | Savings deposits of rural commune members |
		Total	Of which: fixed term deposits	
1952	860	860	480	—
1953	1,230	1,220	680	100
1954	1,590	1,430	980	160
1955	1,990	1,690	1,330	300
1956	2,670	2,240	1,560	430
1957	3,520	2,790	1,960	730
1958	5,520	3,510	2,390	2,010
1959	6,830	4,730	3,160	2,100
1960	6,630	5,110	3,730	1,520
1961	5,540	3,920	2,970	1,620
1962	4,110	3,140	2,560	970
1963	4,570	3,560	2,940	1,010
1964	5,550	4,480	3,700	1,070
1965	6,520	5,230	4,340	1,290
1966	7,230	5,770	4,690	1,460
1967	7,390	5,980	4,890	1,410
1968	7,830	6,230	5,030	1,600

TABLE 12 (Cont'd)
Individual Savings Deposits in China (in million yuan)/a

Year	Total savings deposits	Urban savings deposits		Savings deposits of rural commune members
		Total	Of which: fixed term deposits	
1969	7,590	6,100	4,940	1,490
1970	7,950	6,450	5,380	1,500
1971	9,030	7,330	6,140	1,700
1972	10,520	8,510	6,960	2,010
1973	12,120	9,410	7,770	2,710
1974	13,650	10,580	8,670	3,070
1975	14,960	11,460	9,450	3,500
1976	15,910	12,220	10,060	3,690
1977	18,160	13,510	11,170	4,650
1978	21,060	15,490	12,890	5,570
1979	28,100	20,260	16,640	7,840
1980	39,950	28,250	22,860	11,700
1981	52,370	35,410	28,940	16,960
1982	67,540	44,730	n.a.	22,810

/a Figures are rounded off to the nearest Y 10 million.

Source: State Statistical Bureau (1982), p. 401; Tables 1 and 3.

TABLE 13
Average Per Capita Individual Savings Deposits (in yuan)

Year	In China as a whole		In urban areas		In rural areas	
	Total savings deposits/a	Incremental savings deposits/b	Total savings deposits/a	Incremental savings deposits/b	Total savings deposits/a	Incremental savings deposits/b
1952	1.50	—	12.01	—	—	—
1957	5.44	1.32	28.04	5.53	1.33	0.55
1965	8.99	1.34	42.67	7.37	2.07	0.35
1975	16.27	1.42	102.59	7.88	4.33	0.53
1978	21.98	3.03	129.15	16.51	6.65	1.10
1979	28.94	7.25	157.52	37.09	9.31	2.70
1980	40.66	12.06	210.62	59.57	13.79	4.55
1981	52.57	12.47	255.30	51.62	19.78	6.13
1982	66.52	14.94	n.a.	n.a.	n.a.	n.a.

/a Year-end savings deposits divided by year-end population.
/b Increase in savings deposits during the year divided by year-end population.

Source: Table 12, ZGJJNJ (1981), p. VI-3 and (1982), p. VIII-3.

TABLE 14
Private Financial Savings as a Proportion of
National Income (in %)

Year	Increment in savings deposits divided by national income /a
1957	0.9
1962	-1.5
1965	0.7
1975	0.5
1978	1.0
1979	2.1
1980	3.2
1981	3.2
1982	3.6

/a   The denominator is net material product (the net
     output value of material-producing sectors of the
     economy), based on unadjusted official statistics.

Source: Table 12 and State Statistical Bureau (1982),
          p. 20.   State Statistical Bureau Communique,
          4/29/83; translated in BBC FE7323, 5/3/83,
          p. C12.

TABLE 15
Urban Savings Rates (in %)

Year	Increment in urban savings deposits divided by total wage bill
1977	2.5
1978	3.5
1979	7.4
1980	10.3
1981	8.7
1982	10.6

Source: Table 12. State Statistical Bureau (1982), p. 422. State Statistical Bureau Communique, 6/27/79; translated in BBC FE6153, 6/28/79, p. C1/5. State Statistical Bureau Communique, 4/30/80; translated in BJR, No. 20, 5/19/80, p. 23. State Statistical Bureau Communique, 4/29/83; translated in BBC FE7323, 5/3/83, p. C11.

TABLE 16
Rural Savings Rates (in %)

	Increment in rural savings deposits divided by total rural income /a
1978	0.8
1979	1.7
1980	2.4
1981	2.7

/a Total rural income is obtained by multiplying average per capita peasant income from survey data by rural population. This is likely to be an overestimate for two reasons. The per capita income figures are most likely biased upward (see Travers, 1982), and the rural population figures undoubtedly include many people who do not deposit their money at the rural credit cooperatives but rather at the PBC or other banks (for instance, rural government officials, cadres, perhaps teachers, etc.). Thus the estimated savings rates are too low. Moreover, these figures may understate the increase in the savings rate if reporting of income in the surveys became more complete over time (this would cause an upward bias in the growth rate of average per capita income).

Source: Table 12; ZGJJNJ (1981), p. VI-3 and (1982), p. VIII-3; State Statistical Bureau (1982), p. 431.

TABLE 17
Source of Financing of State Capital Construction Investment
(in billion yuan, current prices)/a

	1965	1975	1978	1979	1980	1981	Difference between 1981 result and revised 1981 plan
National budget	15.4	31.8	39.6	36.2/c	28.1	20.8	
Percent of total	90.1%	81.1%	82.5%	72.4%	52.1%	48.6%	2.1%
Foreign loans /b	0	0	0	2.8	5.4	3.5	
Percent of total	0	0	0	5.6%	10.0%	8.2%	16.8%
Domestic bank loans	0	0	0	0.5	4.1	4.5	
Percent of total	0	0	0	1.0%	7.6%	10.5%	19.2%

TABLE 17 (Cont'd)
Source of Financing of State Capital Construction Investment
(in billion yuan, current prices)/a

	1965	1975	1978	1979	1980	1981	Difference between 1981 result and revised 1981 plan
Local governments and enterprises	1.7	7.4	8.4	10.5	16.4	14.1	
Percent of total	9.9%	18.9%	17.5%	21.0%	30.4%	32.9%	47.8%
Total state capital construction investment	17.1	39.2	48.0	50.0	53.9	42.8	12.6%

/a Detail may not add up to totals due to rounding.
/b Figures refer only to foreign loans incorporated in the state budget. It is possible that foreign loans financed a small amount of investment in 1978.
/c Derived as a residual based on other figures in the same column.

Source: ZGJJNJ (1981), pp. IV-9 and VI-20 and (1982), pp. V-297 and VIII-23.

Abbreviations of Periodicals

BBC   -   British Broadcasting Corporation Summary of
World Broadcasts: China and the Far East
BJR   -   Beijing Review
CBR   -   China Business Review
CMJJ   -   Caimao Jingji (Finance and Trade Economics)
CWKJ   -   Caiwu yu Kuaiji (Finance and Accounting)
CZ   -   Caizheng (State Finance)
FBIS   -   Foreign Broadcast Information Service:
China
JJDB   -   Jingji Daobao (Economic Reporter)
JJGL   -   Jingji Guanli (Economic Management)
JJYJ   -   Jingji Yanjiu (Economic Research)
JPRS   -   Joint Publications Research Service China
Report: Agriculture (AGR); Economic
Affairs (EC); Translations from Red Flag
(RF).
RMRB   -   Renmin Ribao (People's Daily)
RS   -   Radio Service
ZGBKNJ   -   Zhongguo Baike Nianjian (China Encyclopedic
Yearbook)
ZGJJNJ   -   Zhongguo Jingji Nianjian (China Economic
Yearbook)
ZGJR   -   Zhongguo Jinrong (China's Finance)
ZGSHKX   -   Zhongguo Shehui Kexue (Social Sciences in
China)

Note: Except for a few important articles or those
that have been translated into English, all
references to Chinese language materials give
only the periodical number, date, and page
number. For translated materials the page
number given refers to the translation, not the
original.

Notes

CHAPTER 1

1. The two most important journals specializing in discussion of financial aspects are Caizheng (State Finance) and Zhongguo Jinrong (China's Finance). Two other periodicals that often contain useful information are Caiwu yu Kuaiji (Finance and Accounting) and Caimao Jingji (Finance and Trade Economics). The pre-eminent general economics journals, Jingji Yanjiu (Economic Research) and Jingji Guanli (Economic Management) also contain articles on financial issues. There are numerous provincial and local economics journals now available.

CHAPTER 2

1. The general institutional discussion that follows is based mainly on these sources: PBC, Planning Bureau (1980), pp. 2-4; CBR, July-August 1980, pp. 15-18; and Zhang Enhua (1981), p. 26.
2. "The Law of the People's Republic of China on Joint Ventures Using Chinese and Foreign Investment," Article 3; translated in BJR, No. 29, 7/20/79, p. 24. The FICC has since been placed under the jurisdiction of the expanded Ministry of Foreign Trade and Foreign Economic Relations.
3. ZGJR, No. 2, 5/30/79, p. 15.
4. Ibid, and NCNA 7/9/79, in BBC FE6168, 7/16/79, p. BII/1.
5. ZGJR, No. 1, 4/30/79, pp. 15, 17.
6. CBR, July-August 1980, p. 17.
7. NCNA 11/30/79; translated in BBC FE 6291, 12/7/79, p. C1. Zhang Chongfu (1980), p. 75.

8. For a brief discussion on how the Soviet Union developed the concept of a monobank, see Garvy (1977), pp. 18-23. Also see Podolski (1973-1), Chapter 2, for comments on how the banking system came to play an integral role in the Soviet model.

9. Zeng Kanglin and Yan Yi (1980), p. 46.

10. ZGJR, No. 3, 3/30/80, p. 40. Chinese currency is under the decimal system, with the principal unit called the yuan or renminbi. In this book amounts in Chinese currency are always preceded by a "Y." Prices in US dollars were obtained by conversion at the 1980 average exchange rate of Y 1.4984 to 1 US dollar (reported in BJR, No. 29, 7/20/81, p. 22). Since then the foreign exchange value of the yuan has been falling, so procurement prices of gold and other precious metals in US dollars also have fallen.

11. Shanghai City RS, 6/11/80; translated in JPRS EC, No. 67, 7/2/80, p. 42. For 1950s prices see Donnithorne (1967), p. 417.

12. PBC, Planning Bureau (1980), p. 6.

13. CBR, July-August 1980, p. 17.

14. Li Shijing (1979), p. 31.

15. ZGBKNJ (1980), p. 54.

16. ZGJR, No. 24, 12/19/82, p. 36.

17. If it is assumed that all loans to state farms are for circulating capital and all loans to rural communes and brigades are for fixed investment, then about 91% of all loans outstanding at the end of 1981 were of the former type.

18. NCNA 3/7/81; translated in BBC FE6670, 3/11/81, p. C4/3.

19. Wang Bingqian (1980), p. 62.

20. Growth rate based on figures for total loans excluding money advanced to the MOF, from Table 1 and International Financial Statistics, November 1982, pp. 120-121.

21. Li Shijing (1979), p. 33; ZGJR, No. 4, 4/30/80, p. 17.

22. Chen Haowu (1980), p. 9.

23. Yu Ruixiang (1980), p. 51.

24. Hsiao (1971), p. 19; Miyashita (1966), p. 112. For a detailed account of the currencies and banking institutions in Communist-controlled areas before liberation, see pp. 1-54 in Miyashita.

25. Hsiao (1971), p. 27.

26. Cassou (1973), p. 85.

27. Wilson (1980), p. 19.

28. ZGJR, No. 1, 4/30/79, pp. 15, 17. Unless other references are made, the following discussion of the basic role of the ABC is based on this decree.

29. NCNA 2/12/81; translated in BBC FE6650,
2/16/81, p. C2.
30. Miyashita (1966), p. 234.
31. RMRB, 1/28/64, p. 1.
32. The lower figure is from Fang Nie (1980),
p. 73, the higher one from NCNA 10/10/79, in FBIS
10/10/79, p. L13. Since Fang Nie is manager of the
ABC, the former report is likely to be more accurate.
33. According to one report, in Guangxi
agricultural banks were restored in 1980 (Guangxi
Regional RS, 1/5/81; translated in BBC W1121, 2/18/81,
p. A5).
34. Fang Nie (1980), p. 73.
35. ZGBKNJ (1980), p. 298.
36. Hsiao (1971), Table III-3, p. 53.
37. Ibid, pp. 38-41, 48.
38. NCNA 3/2/79; translated in BBC FE6061,
3/8/79, p. BII/11. Like the current incarnation, the
1963-1965 ABC was directly subordinate to the State
Council (Donnithorne, 1967, p. 408).
39. Hsiao (1971), pp. 48-50.
40. For a discussion of the establishment and
development of rural credit cooperatives in the 1950s
and 1960s see Miyashita (1966), Chapter VIII, and
Hsiao (1971), pp. 50-63.
41. Ge Zhida (1980), pp. 8-9.
42. Xinjiang Regional RS, 1/11/81; translated in
JPRS EC, No. 116, 2/10/81, p. 72.
43. State Council circular, 9/22/80; translated
in CBR, November-December 1980, p. 45.
44. ZGJR, No. 2, 5/30/79, p. 15.
45. State Council (1980-1), articles 4, 5,
and 9.
46. China Trade Report, May 1981, p. 5.
47. Hsin Wan Bao (Hong Kong), 12/12/80, p. 2;
translated in JPRS EC, No. 108, 1/14/81, p. 20.
48. China Trade Report, May 1981, p. 5.
49. CBR, July-August 1980, p. 11.
50. China Trade Report, December 1980, p. 7.
51. BOC (1980), p. 17.
52. Guangzhou City RS, 12/13/79; translated in
JPRS EC, No. 39, 1/25/80, p. 36. Also China Trade
Report, May 1980, p. 8.
53. China Trade Report, May 1981, p. 5.
54. Wilczynski (1978), pp. 48-49.
55. ZGBKNJ (1982), pp. 278-279.
56. ZGJJNJ (1982), p. V-341.
57. BJR, No. 29, 7/20/81, p. 22; ZGJR, No. 5,
3/4/82, p. 49; ZGJR, No. 24, 12/19/82, p. 36.
58. Wang Bingqian (1980), p. 68.
59. CBR, July-August 1980, p. 10. Also see Da
Gong Bao, 9/9/80, p. 1; translated in JPRS EC, No. 90,
10/7/80, pp. 1-2.

60. Hsiao (1971), p. 123. It was given the name "Bank of China" only in 1912 (Miyashita, 1966, p.124).
61. State Council circular, 9/22/80; translated in CBR, November-December 1980, p.45.
62. Hsiao (1971), p.23.
63. PBC, Planning Bureau (1980), pp. 2-3.
64. BJR, No. 4, 1/26/81, pp. 25-28.
65. NCNA 7/9/79; in BBC FE6168, 7/16/79, p. BII/1.
66. CBR, September-October 1979, p. 4.
67. "Law of the People's Republic of China on Joint Ventures using Chinese and Foreign Investment," Article 3; in BBC FE6163, 7/10/79, p.C23.
68. NCNA 10/6/79; in BBC FE6238, 10/6/79, p. C1.
69. China Trade Report, August 1981, p. 5.
70. NCNA 1/29/80; in JPRS EC, No. 46, 2/28/80, p. 43.
71. China Trade Report, August 1981, p. 5.
72. Song Guohua (1980-2), p. 8.
73. Zhang Chongfu (1980), p. 75.
74. Song Guohua (1980-2), p. 8.
75. PBC, Planning Bureau (1980), p. 3; Donnithorne (1967), p. 515.
76. Miyashita (1966), pp. 122-123.
77. Song Guohua (1980-1), p. 26.
78. 1978 figure from Song Guohua (1980-1), p. 26.
79. Lower figures from Zhang Chongfu (1980), p. 76; the higher ones are quoted in CBR, March-April 1981, p. 37.
80. ZGJR, No. 1, 1/30/80, p. 9.
81. Song Guohua (1980-1), p. 26.
82. NCNA 12/28/80; translated in JPRS EC, No. 109, 1/15/81, p. 45.
83. ZGJJNJ (1982), p. V-337.
84. Jilin Provincial RS, 8/16/80; translated in JPRS EC, No. 80, 9/2/80, p. 52. Also see ZGJR, No. 1, 1/4/81, p. 48.
85. NCNA 2/28/81; in JPRS EC, No. 122, 3/19/81, p. 2.
86. ZGJR, No. 10, 10/30/80, p. 6.
87. See Donnithorne (1967), pp. 365-366, and CBR, July-August 1980, pp. 16-17.
88. State Council (1980-2), pp. 38-39. Also ZGBKNJ (1980), p. 53.
89. Wang Bingqian (1980), p. 51.
90. Ibid, pp. 51-57.
91. CBR, July-August 1980, p. 17.
92. See Donnithorne (1972), Lardy (1975 and 1978), and the debate between the two authors in The China Quarterly, No. 66, June 1976.
93. Chen, Nai-ruenn (1967), p. 93.

94. Zhou Chuan (1981), p. 4.
95. CMJJ, No. 4, 4/20/82, p.34.
96. PBC, Planning Bureau (1980), p.3.
97. Miyashita (1966), p. 117. Also see PCBC (1978), pp. 233-255.
98. ZGJJNJ (1982), p. V-343.
99. NCNA 11/26/79, reported in CBR, July-August 1980, p. 17. The State Capital Construction Commission has since been absorbed by the State Planning Commission and State Economic Commission.
100. Zhang Enhua (1981), pp. 26-27.
101. ZGJJNJ (1982), p. V-344.
102. Hsiao (1971), pp. 29-32.
103. CBR, July-August 1980, p. 17.
104. Donnithorne (1967), p. 411; Luo Rucheng and Shu Jinzhong (1979).
105. PCBC (1978), pp. 456-458.
106. Ibid, p. 450; Cai Yanchu (1979), p. 47.

CHAPTER 3

1. This discussion is based mainly on the following sources: Podolski (1973-1), pp. 24-57; Wilczynski (1978), pp. 30-31; Garvy (1977), Chapters 4, 5, and 6; and Hsiao (1971), pp. 65-87.
2. According to Hsiao, in the 1950s in China the allowable quota of currency that a unit could retain was equivalent to three days' normal cash expenditures, if that unit was located in an area with a PBC branch (Hsiao, 1971, p. 67).
3. The dual objectives of socialist bank control are described succinctly in Podolski (1973-1), pp. 47-48.
4. Ibid, p. 42.
5. Hsiao (1971), p. 78.
6. Garvy (1977), p. 114.
7. See Kuschpeta (1978), pp. 170-176, for a discussion of cash planning in the USSR.
8. Derived from the statement that 80% of urban savings deposits and 66% of rural savings at the end of 1980 were fixed deposits (NCNA, 1/30/81; in BBC W1120, 2/11/81, p. A5), combined with 1980 year-end balances for urban and rural savings deposits from Table 12.
9. Podolski (1973-2).
10. Kuschpeta (1978), p. 184.
11. Chen Haowu (1980), p. 9.
12. Hsiao (1971), Table II-1, p. 35.
13. State Statistical Bureau (1982), p. 204.
14. ZGJJNJ (1982), p. VIII-26.

172

15. Kornai (1979) provides an insightful
discussion of chronic excess demand in the state
sector of a centrally-planned economy.
16. For a careful summary of the official Chinese
approach to price formation, followed by a
demonstration that it has not been followed in actual
practice, see Wang, Tong-eng (1980), Chapter IV.
17. The most dramatic example of a reduction in
interest rates to maintain price stability in recent
years was the government action in 1978 to reduce
interest rates on circulating capital loans to
grain-trading enterprises by 50 percent.
18. For a discussion of the origin and significance of bank credit fund appropriations, see Hsiao
(1971), pp. 214-217.
19. Hsiao (1971), p. 207.
20. Ibid, pp. 209-212.
21. Wang, Tong-eng (1980), pp. 123-126.
22. Tsakok (1979), p. 865.
23. Liu Mingfu (1979), p. 72.
24. NCNA 6/17/80; translated in FBIS, 6/18/80,
p. L7.
25. NCNA 1/17/81; in BBC W1118, 1/28/81, p. A5.
26. The following discussion is based on Luo
Rucheng and Shu Jinzhong (1979).
27. PCBC (1978), pp. 456-458.
28. Ibid, pp. 450, 454.
29. Cai Yanchu (1979), p. 47.
30. PCBC (1978), p. 451.
31. ZGJR, No. 24, 12/19/82, p. 36. The figures
include some loans made by the BOC and ABC.
32. NCNA 3/21/81; in BBC W1114, 5/20/81, p. A10.
33. Mentioned in Shanghai's Jiefang Ribao
(Liberation Daily), 6/30/80, p. 2; translated in JPRS
EC, No. 80, pp. 72-73.
34. ZGJR, No. 3, 3/30/80, p. 18.
35. Zhongguo Nongmin Bao (China Peasant
Newspaper), 1/18/81, p. 2; translated in JPRS AGR, No.
132, 4/8/81, pp. 1-3. Also see NCNA 8/19/80;
translated in JPRS EC, No. 80, 9/2/80, pp. 8-11.
Also NCNA 8/13/80; in JPRS EC, No. 86, 9/22/80,
pp. 88-89.
36. For example, see Gansu Provincial RS,
11/8/79; translated in BBC W1062, 12/19/79, p. A1.
37. NCNA 8/2/81; in BBC FE6795, 8/7/81,
p. BII/25. The monthly interest rate for loans to
these units was set at 0.33 percent.
38. These figures are derived from data in
Table 1, under the assumption that all loans to rural
communes and production brigades were for fixed
investment; therefore they are undoubtedly biased
downward.

39. ZGJJNJ (1981), p. VI-18 and (1982),
p. VIII-21. Figures refer to state-owned industrial
enterprises which are independent accounting units.
40. Shijie Jingji Daobao (World Economic
Reporter), No. 40, 7/6/81, p. 1; translated in FBIS
8/7/81, pp. K21-K22.
41. Duan Yun (1980), pp. 29, 30.
42. ZGJR, Nos. 11-12, 11/30/80, p. 37 provides
these percentages for commercial, material supply, and
foreign trade enterprises.
43. Ma Hong and Sun Shangqing (1982), pp. 39,80;
ZGJJNJ (1981), p. IV-9; Wang Bingqian (1982), p.
C2/7.
44. State Statistical Bureau (1982), p. 232.
45. Wen Hui Bao, 1/29/81, p. 3; translated in
JPRS EC, No. 120, 3/16/81, p. 11.
46. RMRB, 3/2/81, p. 5; translated in JPRS EC,
No. 130, 4/15/81, p. 8.
47. Wang Bingqian (1982), p. C2/7.
48. 1980 export figure from State Statistical
Bureau Communique, in BJR, No. 20, 5/18/81, p. 18;
inventory figure from Duan Yun (1980), p. 34.
49. Cai Bianwen (1979), p. 39; Yi Hongren
(1979), p. 2.
50. Wan Jung (1979), p. 2.
51. NCNA 4/11/79; translated in BBC W1030,
5/9/79, pp. A4-A5.
52. ZGJR, No. 3, 3/30/80, p. 19.

CHAPTER 4

1. Some of the main goals of this plan as well
as the underlying ideology are expressed in Hua
Guofeng (1978).
2. Lenin, quoted in Hu Qiaomu (1978), p. BII/14.
3. See He Jianzhang (1980).
4. State Council (1980-2).
5. The earlier decentralization is described in
Lardy (1978), pp. 90-99.
6. CBR, March-April 1980, p. 20 and
September-October 1980, p. 11.
7. Deng Jie et al (1980).
8. Wu Qiyu (1980).
9. NCNA 5/29/81; in BBC FE6753, 6/19/81,
p. BII/4.
10. The success of this campaign is described
briefly in ZGJR, No. 1, 4/30/79, p. 1.
11. The emphasis was on sales drives by enterprises themselves and their parent bureaus to get rid
of inventories. See Wan Jung (1979), p. 7.

174

12. NCNA 10/15/78; translated in BBC FE5947, 10/20/78, p. 7.

13. For instance, see BBC FE5950, 10/24/78, p. BII/18 and FE5926, 9/26/78, p. BII/1.

14. ZGJR, No. 2, 5/30/79, p. 1. The summary of minutes of the meeting is translated in the same issue, pp. 1-4.

15. ZGBKNJ (1980), pp. 297-298.

16. ZGJR, No. 1, 4/30/79, pp. 15, 17.

17. ZGJR, No. 2, 5/30/79, p. 15.

18. ZGJR, No. 1, 4/30/79, p. 22.

19. ZGJR, No. 1, 4/30/79, p. 15, and No. 2, 5/30/79, p. 15.

20. ZGJR, No. 2, 2/29/80, p. 27.

21. ZGJR, Nos. 11-12, 11/30/80, p. 9.

22. ZGJR, No. 24, 12/19/82, p. 10.

23. NCNA 11/30/79; translated in BBC FE6291, 12/7/79, pp. C1-C2.

24. NCNA 7/8/79; in BBC FE6163, 7/10/79, pp. C22-C26.

25. NCNA 10/4/79; in BBC FE6238, 10/6/79, p. C1. Also see NCNA 7/9/79; in BBC FE6168, 7/16/79, p. BII/1. An interview given by Rong Yiren, CITIC's president and Chairman of the Board of Directors, appeared in CBR, September-October 1979, pp. 4-6. In it he mentions having discussions with foreigners "during the past few months."

26. NCNA 9/19/78; in BBC, 10/4/78, p. A9. ZGBKNJ (1982), pp. 278-279.

27. BOC (1980), p. 17; ZGJJNJ (1982), p. V-341.

28. For example, in 1979 in Heilongjiang Province 5,350 PBC cadres, or 41.2 percent of the total number, underwent training (ZGJR, No. 3, 3/30/81, p. 12).

29. An article on financial institutes of higher education appeared in ZGJR, No. 1, 1/4/81, pp. 16-19.

30. NCNA 12/30/79; in JPRS EC, No. 39, 1/25/80, p. 8.

31. For example, the college of finance and economics in Jiangxi Province in 1979 started offering 5 month courses for county-level financial bureau chiefs from all over China, with the support of the Ministry of Finance (NCNA 9/13/79; in JPRS EC, No. 21, 10/16/79, p. 17).

32. NCNA 11/16/79; translated in BBC FE6279, 11/23/79, pp. C1/1-C1/2.

33. ZGJJNJ (1981), p. II-138.

34. NCNA 11/26/79; translated in BBC FE6279, 11/23/79, pp. C1/1, C1/2.

35. ZGJJNJ (1982), p. V-344.

36. Shanghai City RS, 2/25/81; translated in BBC FE6663, 3/3/81, p. BII/16.

37. Gongren Ribao (Workers' Daily), 11/7/80, p. 1; translated in JPRS EC, No. 116, 2/10/81, p. 70.

38. This brief outline of the points raised at the meeting is based on ZGJR, No. 3, 3/30/80, pp. 4-5.

39. State Council (1981), pp. C1/1, C1/4-C1/5.

40. He Jianzhang (1981), title.

41. The difficulties mentioned in this paragraph are discussed in ZGJR, Nos. 11-12, 11/30/80, p. 20.

42. ZGJR, Nos. 11-12, 11/30/80, p. 9. Also same issue, p. 7.

43. NCNA 2/12/81; translated in BBC FE6650, 2/16/80, p. C2.

44. ZGJR, No. 1, 1/4/81, p. 11.

45. NCNA 2/12/81; translated in BBC FF6650, 2/16/81, p. C2.

46. ZGJR, No. 2, 2/29/80, p. 22.

47. ZGJR, No. 9, 9/30/80, p. 23.

48. NCNA 2/12/81; translated in BBC FE6650, 2/16/81, p. C1.

49. ZGJR, No. 4, 4/30/80, p. 18.

50. ZGJR, Nos. 11-12, 11/30/80, pp. 5-7, 9. NCNA 4/20/81; translated in BBC FE6709, 4/28/81, pp. BII/20-BII/21.

51. NCNA 4/20/81; translated in BBC FE6709, 4/28/81, p. BII/21.

52. NCNA 2/3/81; translated in BBC FE6643, 2/7/81, pp. C1-C2. The following summary is greatly condensed and paraphrases the original.

53. State Council (1981).

54. ZGJR, No. 3, 3/30/80, p. 18.

55. ZGJR, No. 10, 10/30/80, p. 6.

56. ZGJJNJ (1982), p. V-321.

57. See Vice Premier Yao Yilin's speech of 2/25/81, in ZGJJNJ (1982), p. II-46.

58. ZGJJNJ (1982), p. II-58.

59. Wang Bingqian (1982), p. C2/1.

60. The following summary is based on NCNA 2/12/81; translated in BBC FE6650, 2/16/81, pp. C1-C3.

CHAPTER 5

1. ZGJR, Nos. 11-12, 11/30/80, p. 9 and No. 2, 2/29/80, p. 27. Also see ZGJR, No. 24, 12/19/82, p. 10.

2. ZGJR, No. 2, 2/29/80, p. 27.

3. See ZGJR, No. 12, 6/19/82, p. 19. In ZGJR, Nos. 11-12, 11/30/80, p. 10, it was suggested that bank branches should be allowed to make additional short- and medium-term equipment loans if they attract more deposits, but it is doubtful whether this idea was implemented before 1982.

4. If the bank receives one unit of additional
deposits it will be able to make a new loan of one
unit. This in turn will cause deposits to increase
by x units, allowing a further increase in loans of
that amount. The third round effect will allow an
increase in loans of x squared, and so on. Thus the
total allowable increase in loans resulting from a
unit increase in deposits is: $1+x+x^2+x^3+... = \dfrac{1}{1-x}$

5. For the purposes of this exercise it is
assumed that the entire surplus of deposits over
loans of rural credit cooperatives is included in the
figures in Table 1 under the category "deposits in
rural areas." In deriving the value of x for urban
areas the increment in loans for advance purchases,
to state farms, and to rural communes and brigades
was subtracted from the increment in total loans,
resulting in a rough indication of the increase in
loans in urban areas.

6. According to Hsiao total deposits in the
PBC at the end of 1957 were Y 20.92 billion, while
loans outstanding at the same time totalled Y 28.7
billion (Hsiao, 1971, pp. 125, 162).

7. Liaoning figures are from Liaoning Ribao
(Liaoning Daily), 5/15/81; translated in BBC W1138,
6/17/81, pp. C1 and C6. China's 1980 national income
was reported in BJR, No. 19, 5/11/81, p. 23; the
currency figure is from Table 1.

8. Of course this is an increase in "inside
money" offset by increases in assets of the banking
system (loans outstanding). Outside money (currency
in circulation) remains unchanged.

9. ZGJR, No. 2, 1/19/82, p. 6.

10. For example, see Qiye Guanli (Enterprise
Management), No. 5, 9/1/82, pp. 21-22.

11. Hsiao (1971), p. 152.

12. PBC, Planning Bureau (1980), pp. 7-8,
modified by ZGJR, No. 9, 9/30/80, p. 16.

13. Derived from the statement that 80 percent of
urban savings deposits and 66 percent of rural savings
at the end of 1980 were fixed deposits (NCNA, 1/30/81;
in BBC W1120, 2/11/81, p. A5), combined with 1980
year-end balances for urban and rural savings deposits
from Tables 1 and 3.

14. NCNA 3/14/81; in BBC W1132, 5/6/81, p. A16.
JJYJ, No. 6, 6/20/80, p. 30.

15. ZGJR, No. 3, 3/30/80, p. 18.

16. Interest payments were calculated by taking
5.04 percent of the 1980 year-end balance of loans
oustanding to state industrial production enterprises
and for equipment purchases (Table 1). This may
overestimate interest payments, since not all short-
and medium-term equipment loans were received by

industrial enterprises. Output value figure is from
State Statistical Bureau (1982), p. 208.
    17. ZGJR, No. 4, 4/30/80, p. 17.
    18. For instance, see ZGJR, Nos. 11-12, 11/30/80,
p. 18.
    19. China Trade Report, August 1981, p. 5.
    20. Gongren Ribao (Workers' Daily), 2/13/81;
translated in JPRS EC, No. 117, 2/13/81, pp. 12-13.
Ma Hong (1980), p. 22.
    21. The following discussion is based mainly on
an article in ZGJR, No. 8, 8/30/80, pp. 18-19.
    22. Speech by Premier Zhao Ziyang at the national
conference on industry and transport, 3/4/82; translated in BBC FE6994, 4/2/82, p. C1/12.
    23. This list is based on the description of the
Tianjin Trust and Investment Corporation in ZGJR,
No. 10, 10/30/80, p. 6.
    24. ZGJR, No. 10, 10/30/80, p. 6. It is likely
that these rates were raised when interest rates on
bank deposits of enterprises and organizations were
increased in 1982.
    25. Ibid. Loan rates were probably raised in
1982.
    26. ZGBKNJ (1982), p. 282. The figures most
likely include trust offices within banks as well as
trust and investment corporations.
    27. State Statistical Bureau (1982, p. 403).
Growth rates are calculated on the basis of average
price levels during each year (not the year-end
index). The retail price index is a weighted average
of the index of official prices, negotiated prices,
and free market prices.
    28. Hongqi (Red Flag), No. 8, 4/16/82, p. 27.
    29. Li Chengrui (1981), p. 30.
    30. Lin Jiken (1981), pp. 83-84.
    31. State Statistical Bureau Communique, in BJR,
No. 19, 5/11/81, p. 23.
    32. Lin Jiken (1981), pp. 85-86, provides some
interesting insights into how currency issuance
resulting from credit as opposed to budget deficits
can also be inflationary.
    33. Hsiao (1971), pp. 209-212.

CHAPTER 6

    1. These growth rates are based on figures in
the following sources: State Statistical Bureau
Communique, 6/27/79, in BBC FE6153, 6/28/79, p. C1/5;
ZGJJNJ (1981), pp. VI-7, VI-8 and (1982), p. VIII-7;
and State Statistical Bureau (1982), p. 329.

2. State Statistical Bureau (1982), p. 409.
3. One example is the following passage in a
letter from a peasant in Hebei. "Our commune has
more than 4,000 peasant households. But only a few
dozen bicycles are allocated to our commune for sale
each year. If 1,000 bicycles and 1,000 sewing
machines were put on sale in our commune, they would
be sold out in no time." (NCNA 3/11/81; in BBC
FE6673, 3/14/81, p. BII/12).
4. ZGJJNJ (1982), p. VIII-3; State Statistical
Bureau (1982), pp. 329, 431.
5. ZGJR, No. 6, 9/30/79, p. 14.
6. Li Chengrui (1981), p. 34.
7. China Daily, 6/6/81, p. 1. According to a
different source, the number of joint ventures
approved by China's Foreign Investment Control
Commission as of early 1981 was 24 (CBR, March-April
1981, pp. 22-23). Unless otherwise specified, the
rest of the information in this paragraph (including
the quoted passage) comes from the China Daily
article.
8. BJR, No. 16, 4/20/81, p. 16.
9. Based on the assumption that the ratio of
foreign to total investment is roughly the same as
that reported in CBR, March-April 1981, p. 22, for
December 1980.
10. BJR, No. 16, 4/20/81, p. 16.
11. For example, see Chen Xuecheng (1980).
12. Ibid. Also Da Gong Bao (Hong Kong), 12/2/80,
p. 5, translated in JPRS EC, No. 107, 1/9/81, p. 102.
13. China's trade surplus of Y 5.66 billion in
1982 means that equipment imports can be increased
without nontrade financing (State Statistical Bureau
Communique, 4/29/83, in BBC FE7323, 4/29/83, p. C9).
14. According to preliminary estimates, in 1982
the national budget accounted for only 37 percent of
total capital construction investment (RMRB, 12/20/83,
p. 2).
15. NCNA 3/7/81; translated in BBC FE6670,
3/11/81, p. C4/7.
16. Shanxi Ribao (Shanxi Daily), 3/28/81;
translated in BBC W1136, 6/3/81, pp. A13-A14.
17. Donnithorne (1967), pp. 389-390.
18. NCNA 12/19/78; translated in BBC FE6007,
1/4/79, p. BII/16.
19. For an interesting account of the development
of collective enterprises in a single municipality see
Xiao Liang et al (1980). In 1978 or 1979 the profits
of large collective enterprises under the control of
this particular municipality's industrial bureau were
equivalent to 2.6 times the local budgetary income
(p. 28).

20. Donnithorne (1967), pp. 390, 391.
21. Tian Chunsheng (1979), p. 56. See Naughton (1981) for a detailed discussion.
22. Percentages for 1976, 1979, and 1980 from Zhou Chuan (1981), p. 4.
23. Wang Bingqian (1980), p. 66 and (1982), p. C2/2.
24. The following description is based on Wang Guocheng et al (1980).
25. This and the following information is from Beijing Ribao (Peking Daily), 7/29/80, p. 1; translated in JPRS EC, No. 87, 9/26/80, pp. 62-63.
26. Tianjin Ribao (Tianjin Daily), 6/26/80, p. 1; translated in JPRS EC, No. 87, 9/26/80, p. 66.
27. FBIS 6/30/80, p. L17.
28. Sichuan Ribao (Sichuan Daily), 8/5/80, p. 2; translated in JPRS AGR, No. 108, 10/30/80, p. 51.
29. He Jianzhang (1981), p. 15.
30. Ibid, pp. 15-16.
31. NCNA 2/14/81; translated in BBC FE6652, 2/18/81, p. C4.
32. NCNA 6/14/80; translated in FBIS, 6/19/80, p. L15.
33. For example, see RMRB, 7/19/79, p. 1; translated in JPRS EC, No. 13, 9/12/79, pp. 84-85.
34. For example, 20 out of Shanghai's 32 urban-rural joint ventures set up as of June 1980 had estimated payback periods of less than a year (NCNA 6/16/80; in FBIS 6/17/80, p. 02).
35. Lin Senmu and Tan Kewen (1980), p. 74.
36. RMRB 3/2/81, p. 5; translated in JPRS EC, No. 130, 4/15/81, p. 8.
37. Shen Lu et al (1980), p. 112.

CHAPTER 7

1. See Zwass (1979) and Wilczynski (1978). An earlier book whose only defect is that it dates from before the most significant reforms is Garvy (1966). Two other books that deal only with the USSR but nevertheless might prove useful are Garvy (1977) and Kuschpeta (1978).
2. Podolski (1973-1); Dimitrijevic and Macesich (1973); Goldsmith (1975). Also see Hare (1981) and Part VI in Horvat (1976).
3. This discussion is based on Zwass (1979), pp. 94-96 and pp. 146-150.
4. Ibid, pp. 95-96.
5. Wu Qiyu (1980), pp. 57-58.
6. Horvat (1976), p. 209.
7. Ibid, p. 211.

8. Kornai (1979).
9. Zwass (1979), p. 135.
10. Balassa (1978), p. 247.
11. The following discussion of the USSR and Poland is based on Podolski (1973-2).
12. See Tyson (1977 and 1978).
13. Tyson (1977), p. 294.
14. Ibid, pp. 286-287.
15. ZGJR, No. 1, 1/4/81, p. 11.
16. Zwass (1977), p. 23.
17. Balassa (1978), p. 247.
18. Kuschpeta (1978), pp. 45-46, 58.
19. Wilczynski (1978), p. 25.
20. Holzman (1979).
21. Fallenbuchl (1981), pp. 53, 61.
22. Marer (1981), pp. 541-542.

CHAPTER 8

1. See the regulations on short- and medium-term equipment loans in ZGJJNJ (1981), p. II-140.
2. The interest rate on enterprises' three and five year fixed deposits is only slightly higher than the interest paid for Treasury bonds, which are not purchased voluntarily by enterprises.
3. One Chinese textbook on banking explicitly notes that in theory there is the possibility that loans and deposits can feed on each other and grow indefinitely. But any likelihood that this could happen is immediately dismissed, since all bank loans are "guaranteed" by material resources in the possession of the borrower. See Jinrong Jichu Zhishi (1981), p. 31.
4. See ZGJR, No. 2, 2/4/83, p. 16.
5. RMRB, 1/25/83, p. 5.
6. State Council Circular No. 141 (1982), 12/4/82, in Guowuyuan Gongbao (Bulletin of the State Council) No. 21, 2/12/83, pp. 1004-1005.
7. The prohibition against nonbank-related trust organizations was made by Premier Zhao Ziyang in a speech to the national conference on industry and transport, 3/4/82; translated in BBC FE6994, 4/2/82, p. C1/12. Some suggestions on tightening supervision of trust work are made in ZGJR, No. 24, 12/19/82.
8. State Council Circular No. 153 (1982), in Guowuyuan Gongbao (Bulletin of the State Council) No. 21, 2/12/83, p. 1007. The document also stipulates that trust operations not specifically approved by the State Council must be shut down by the end of June 1983.

Bibliography

Balassa, Bela, "The Economic Reform in Hungary, Ten Years After," European Economic Review, 11(3), October 1978, pp. 245-268.

Bank of China (BOC), "Do a good job in Foreign Exchange Work, Promote the Readjustment of the National Economy," ZGJR, No. 3, 3/30/80, pp. 20-21; translated in JPRS EC, No. 82, 9/9/80, pp. 15-20.

Cai Bianwen, "Putting an End to Waste is the Urgent Task in the Realization of the Four Modernizations," CWKJ, No. 7, 7/20/79, pp. 11-15; translated in JPRS EC, No. 30, 11/28/79, pp. 37-46.

Cai Yanchu, "Is the Appropriation of Funds Without Payment at the Crux of the Unduly Long Battlefront in Capital Construction," JJGL, No. 8, 8/25/79, pp. 20-22; translated in JPRS EC, No. 34, 1/2/80, pp. 45-49.

Cassou, Pierre-Henri, "The Chinese Monetary System," Le Bulletin de l'Economie et des Finances, October 1973; translated in Chinese Economic Studies, 9(4), Summer 1976, pp. 82-97.

Chen Haowu, "Some Problems about the Decisionmaking Power of Banks," ZGJR, No. 11-12, 11/30/80, pp. 22-23; translated in JPRS EC, No. 132, 4/27/81, pp. 9-12.

Chen, Nai-Ruenn, Chinese Economic Statistics: A Handbook for Mainland China, Chicago: Aldine Publishing Company, 1967.

Chen Xuecheng, "Tentative Discussion of the Pros and Cons of Compensatory Trade," Guoji Maoyi Wenti (International Trade Questions), No. 3, September 1980, pp. 37-38; translated in JPRS EC, No. 100, 12/2/80, pp. 32-35.

182

Deng Jie, Yao Kaiqi, Cheng Heng, and Shao Yunjie, "A
    Probe into the Establishment of a China
    Industrial and Commercial Credit Bank," JJYJ,
    No. 5, 5/20/80, pp. 54-56; translated in JPRS EC,
    No. 74, 8/5/80, pp. 118-123.
Dimitrijevic, Dimitrije, and Macesich, George, Money
    and Finance in Contempory Yugoslavia; New York:
    Praeger, 1973.
Donnithorne, Audrey, China's Economic System; New
    York: Praeger, 1967.
_____, "China's Cellular Economy; Some Economic Trends
    since the Cultural Revolution," The China
    Quarterly, No. 52, October/December 1972.
Duan Yun, "Certain Questions on Finance, Credit and
    Balanced Supply of Commodities," HQ, No. 17,
    9/1/80, pp. 12-18, 24, and No. 18, 9/16/80,
    pp. 16-22; translated in JPRS RF No. 17, 12/5/80,
    pp. 18-29 and No. 18, 12/10/80, pp. 26-38,
    respectively.
Fallenbuchl, Zbigniew M., "The Polish Economy at the
    Beginning of the 1980s," in US Congress, Joint
    Economic Committee, East European Economic
    Assessment: Part 1 - Country Studies, 1980;
    Washington, D.C.: US Government Printing Office,
    1981; pp. 33-71.
Fang Nie, Interview in JJDB, No. 16, 4/23/80, p.4;
    translated in JPRS AGR, No. 87, 6/26/80,
    pp. 73-75.
Garvy, George, Money, Banking, and Credit in Eastern
    Europe; New York: Federal Reserve Bank of New
    York, 1966.
_____, Money, Financial Flows, and Credit in the
    Soviet Union; Cambridge, MA.: Ballinger
    Publishing Company, 1977.
Ge Zhida, "More Efficient use of Fiscal Agricultural
    Aid Funds," JJYJ, No. 2, 2/20/80, pp. 12-18;
    translated in JPRS AGR, No. 81, 5/2/80, pp. 4-17.
_____ "Discussion on Balancing Revenue and
    Expenditure," JJYJ, No. 1, 1/20/81, pp. 54-60;
    translated in JPRS EC, No. 129, 4/14/81,
    pp. 1-10.
Goldsmith, Raymond W., "The Financial Development of
    Yugoslavia," Banca Nazionale del Lavoro
    Quarterly Review, Vol 28, No. 112, March 1975,
    pp. 61-108.
Hare, P.G., "The Investment System in Hungary," in
    Hare, P.G., Radice, H.K., and Swain, N., eds.,
    Hungary: A Decade of Economic Reform; London:
    George Allen and Unwin, 1981, pp. 83-106.
He Jianzhang, "Newly Emerging Economic Forms," BJR,
    No. 21, 5/25/81, pp. 15-18.

Holzman, Franklyn D., "Some Theories of the Hard
    Currency Shortages of Centrally Planned
    Economies," in US Congress, Joint Economic
    Committee, Soviet Economy in a Time of Change;
    Washington, D.C.: US Government Printing Office,
    1979, pp. 297-316.
Horvat, Branko, The Yugoslav Economic System, The
    First Labor Managed Economy in the Making; White
    Plains, N.Y.: International Arts and Sciences
    Press, 1976.
Hsiao, Katharine Huang, Money and Monetary Policy in
    Communist China; New York: Columbia University
    Press, 1971.
Hu Qiaomu, "Act in Accordance with Economic Laws, Step
    up the Four Modernizations," RMRB 10/6/78; trans-
    lated in BBC FE5939, 10/11/78, pp. BII/1-BII/20.
Hua Guofeng, "Unite and Strive to Build a Modern,
    Powerful Socialist Country" (speech at the First
    Session of the Fifth National People's Congress,
    2/26/78), in Documents of the First Session of
    the Fifth National People's Congress of the
    People's Republic of China; Beijing: Foreign
    Languages Press, 1978.
International Financial Statistics (monthly).
Jinrong Jichu Zhishi; Beijing: China Finance and
    Economics Publishing House, 1981.
Kornai, Janos, "Resource-Constrained versus
    Demand-Constrained Systems," Econometrica 47(4),
    July 1979, pp. 801-819.
Kuschpeta, O., The Banking and Credit System of the
    USSR; Boston: Martinus Nijhoff, 1978.
Lardy, Nicholas R., "Centralization and
    Decentralization in China's Fiscal Management,"
    The China Quarterly, No. 61, March 1975,
    pp. 25-60.
          , Economic Growth and Distribution in China;
    New York: Cambridge University Press, 1978.
Li Chengrui, "The Balance of Finance and Credit in
    Relation to the Overall Balance of the National
    Economy," JJYJ, No. 3, 3/20/81; translated in
    JPRS EC, No. 141, 6/4/81, pp. 29-45.
Li Shijing, "Banking System Should be Changed to
    Vertical Leadership," JJGL, No. 8, 8/25/79,
    pp. 13-14; translated in JPRS EC, No. 34,
    1/2/80, pp. 31-34.
Lin Jiken, "Persist in Issuing Currency in Line with
    Economic Principles," JJYJ, No. 1, 1/20/81,
    pp. 60-63, 78; translated in JPRS EC, No. 135,
    5/11/81, pp. 81-87.
Lin Senmu and Tan Kewen, "On Getting Better Returns
    from Investments," JJYJ, No. 6, 6/20/80,
    pp. 26-32; translated in JPRS EC, No. 81,
    9/3/80, pp. 72-85.

Liu Mingfu, "On the Economic Form of Socialist
Economy," JJYJ, No. 4, 4/20/79; translated in
Chinese Economic Studies, 13(3), Spring 1980,
pp. 69-82.
Luo Rucheng and Shu Jinzhong, "Chongfen Fahui
Xiaoxing Jishu Cuoshi Daikoan de Jiji Zuoyong -
Shanghaishi Xiaoxing Jishu Daikoan Diaocha"
(Bring into Full Play and Enthusiastically Make
Use of Small-scale Loans for Technical Measures -
An Investigation of Shanghai Municipality's
Small-scale Loans for Technical Measures), JJGL,
No. 12, 12/25/79, pp. 28-30.
Ma Hong, "Integration and Competition in the Socialist
Economy, (I)," JJGL, No. 10, 10/15/80, pp. 17-20;
translated in JPRS EC, No. 107, 1/9/81,
pp. 22-28.
_____ and Sun Shangqing, eds., Zhongguo Jingji Jiegou
Wenti Yanjiu (Studies on the Structure of the
Chinese Economy); Beijing: People's Publishing
House, 1982.
Marer, Paul, "Exchange Rates and Convertibility in
Hungary's New Economic Mechanism," in US
Congress, Joint Economic Committee, East European
Economic Assessment; Part I - Country Studies,
1980; Washington, D.C.: US Government Printing
Office, 1981, pp. 525-548.
Miyashita, Tadao, The Currency and Financial System
of Mainland China (translated by J.R. McEwan);
Seattle: University of Washington Press, 1966.
Naughton, Barry, "Financial Resources and Incentives
in Chinese Industry," unpublished paper, 1981.
People's Bank of China (PBC), Planning Bureau,
Financial Overview of the People's Republic of
China, June 1980; translated in JPRS EC, No. 105,
12/24/80, pp. 1-21.
People's Construction Bank of China (PCBC), Jiben
Jianshe Caiwu Bokoan Zhidu Xuanbian (Selections
on the System of Financial Appropriations for
Capital Construction); Beijing: China Finance
and Economics Publishing House, 1978.
Podolski, T.M., Socialist Banking and Monetary
Control, The Experience of Poland; London:
Cambridge University Press, 1973.
_____, "Trade Credit and Monetary Control," in Laulan,
M. Yves, ed., Banking, Money and Credit in
Eastern Europe, Main Findings of a Colloquium
held 24th - 26th January, 1973 in Brussels;
Brussels: NATO, 1973.
Shen Lu, Ke Wen, and Gong Jing, "What are the Reasons
for Low Returns on Capital Construction
Investment?" RMRB, 4/29/80, p.5.; translated in
JPRS EC, No. 70, 7/23/80, pp. 112-117.

Song Guohua, "Development of China's Insurance Business," interview in JJDB, No. 13, 4/2/80, pp. 2-3; translated in JPRS EC, No. 71, 7/22/80, pp. 24-28.

_____, "Fazhan Renmin Baoxian Shiye Wei Sihua Jianshe Fuwu" (Develop People's Insurance Work, Serve the Four Modernizaitons), ZGJR, No. 1, 1/30/80, pp. 7-8, 17.

State Council, "Provisional Regulations for Exchange Control of the People's Republic of China" (12/18/80), in BJR, No. 4, 1/26/81, pp. 25-28.

_____, "The Temporary Provisions for Carrying out a Financial Management System of Apportioning Revenues and Expenditures between the Central and Local Authorities, While Holding the Latter Responsible for their own Profit and Loss." (February 1980), CZ, No. 12, December 1980, pp. 1-2; translated in JPRS EC, No. 120, 3/16/81, pp. 35-39.

_____, "Regulations on Treasury Bonds of the PRC" (1/16/81); translated in BBC FE6670, 3/11/81, p. C1/1.

State Statistical Bureau, Zhongguo Tongji Nanjian 1981 (1981 China Statistical Yearbook); Beijing: China Statistical Publishing House, 1982.

Tian Chunsheng, "The Economic Nature of the Fixed Asset Depreciation Fund," JJGL, No. 2, 2/15/79, pp. 48-51; translated in JPRS EC, No. 5, 8/3/79, pp. 53-59.

Travers, S. Lee, "Bias in Chinese Economic Statistics: The Case of the Typical Example Investigation," The China Quarterly, No. 91, September 1982, pp. 478-485.

Tsakok, Isabelle, "Inflation Control in the People's Republic of China, 1949-1974," World Development 7 (8/9), August-September 1979, pp. 865-876.

Tyson, Laura D'Andrea, "Liquidity Crises in the Yugoslav Economy: An Alternative to Bankruptcy," Soviet Studies, 29(2), April 1977, pp. 284-295.

_____, "Enterprise Demand for Money and Illiquidity Crises in Yugoslavia," European Economic Review, 12(1), February 1979, pp. 53-71.

Wan Jung, "Tap the Potentials from Enterprises, Speed up Turnover of Materials," JJGL, No. 8, 8/25/79, pp. 26-29; translated in JPRS EC, No. 32, 12/10/79, pp. 1-7.

Wang Bingqian, "Report on the Final State Accounts for 1979, the Draft State Budget for 1980 and the Financial Estimates for 1981," in Main Documents of the Third Session of the Fifth National People's Congress of the People's Republic of China; Beijing: Foreign Languages Press, 1980; pp. 48-85.

186

_____, report to the Fifth Session of the Fifth
National People's Congress, December 1982;
translated in BBC FE7209, 12/15/82,
pp. C2/1-C2/10.

Wang Guocheng, Liu Gang, and Xing Yichu, "There is
Great Promise in Joint Industrial and
Agricultural Management - Investigation on the
Shanghai Dazhihe Woolen Mill," JJGL, No. 10,
10/15/80, pp. 37-39; translated in JPRS EC,
No. 107, 1/9/81, pp. 53-58.

Wang, Tong-eng, Economic Policies and Price Stability
in China; Center for Chinese Studies, University
of California, China Research Monograph No. 16;
Berkeley: University of California, 1980.

Wilczynski, J., Comparative Monetary Economics;
London: MacMillan Press, 1978.

Wilson, Dick, "How Banks Work in China," The Banker,
January 1980, pp. 19-27.

Wu Qiyu, "Is Vertical Leadership needed in the Banking
System - A Discussion on the Problem of
Restructuring the Banking System," JJGL, No. 2,
2/15/80, pp. 13-14; translated in JPRS EC, No.
62, 5/20/80, pp. 55-58.

Xiao Liang, Tang Zongkun, and Zhang Tianxin, "The Big
Collective Industries of Weihai Municipality,"
ZGSHKX, No. 1, January 1980, pp. 213-224; trans-
lated in JPRS EC, No. 61, 5/9/80, pp. 18-38.

Xu Yi and Chen Yulin, 1977-1980 Zhongguo Caizheng
(China's Government Finance, 1977-1980); Beijing:
People's Publishing House, 1982.

Yi Hongren, "On the Question of the Circulation Fund
Management System," JJYJ, No. 8, 8/20/79,
pp. 40-44; translated in JPRS EC, No. 31,
12/4/79, pp. 1-9.

Yi Ruixiang, "Several Questions Concerning the
Economic Leverage of Banks," ZGJR, No. 5,
5/30/80, pp. 16-17; translated in JPRS EC,
No. 89, 10/3/80, pp. 49-53.

Yu Guantao, article in Jinrong Yanjiu (Financial
Research), No. 4, 1981, pp. 39-50.

Zeng Kanglin and Yan Yi, "The Present Financial and
Banking System must be Reformed," RMRB, 10/6/80,
p. 5; translated in JPRS EC, No. 103, 12/11/80,
pp. 46-50.

Zhang Chongfu, "Tentative Ideas on Restructuring of
the Insurance System," JJGL, No. 2, 2/15/80,
pp. 15-17; translated in JPRS EC, No. 63,
6/3/80; pp. 75-80.

Zhang Enhua, "On Banking Reform," BJR, No. 29,
7/20/81, pp. 24-27.

Zhongguo Baike Nianjian (ZGBKNJ - Encyclopedic
    Yearbook of China): Beijing and Shanghai:
    Zhongguo Da Baike Quanshu Chubanshe, 1980,
    1981, and 1982.
Zhongguo Jingji Nianjian (ZGJJNJ - China Economic
    Yearbook); Beijing: Jingji Guanli Zazhishe, 1981
    and 1982.
Zhou Chuan, "Continue to Grasp Readjustment Well,
    Stabilize Economic Development," JJGL, No. 1,
    1/15/81, pp. 7-9; translated in JPRS EC, No. 125,
    3/30/81, pp. 1-6.
Zwass, Adam, "The Credit System of the Planned
    Economies in Transformation," Eastern European
    Economics, 15(4), Summer 1977, pp. 17-28.
    Money, Banking and Credit in the Soviet
    Union and Eastern Europe: London: MacMillan,
    1979.